The Beneficiary's Answer Book

Straightforward answers to 175 questions asked most often by beneficiaries of estates

Lynne Butler, BA LLB TEP

Copyright ©2013 by Lynne Butler.

All rights reserved.

No part of this book may be reproduced or transmitted in any form by any means graphic, electronic, or mechanical without permission in writing from the publisher, except by a reviewer who may quote brief passages in a review. Any requests for photocopying, recording, taping or information and retrieval systems of any part of this book shall be directed in writing to the publisher. Contact www.estatelawcanada.com for more information.

Printed in the U.S.A.

First edition: 2013

ISBN 978-1-304-52773-8

Table of Contents

5. Introduction

8. Chapter 1: The will

22. Chapter 2: Probate

29. Chapter 3: Funeral arrangements

35. Chapter 4: Joint property

42. Chapter 5: Beneficiary designations

49. Chapter 6: Your rights as a beneficiary

62. Chapter 7: The executor

74. Chapter 8: Personal and household items

82. Chapter 9: Distribution of the estate

88. Chapter 10: Tax

96. Chapter 11: Trusts

105. Chapter 12: Lawyers

112: Chapter 13: The executor's accounts and Releases

127. Chapter 14: Contesting a will

133. Conclusion

Introduction

There are plenty of books out there that tell a person how to make a will, and even some books that help executors to do their job. But what's out there to let a beneficiary know what to expect, what rights exist, and how to know when something is wrong? Where are beneficiaries to turn to get information?

Almost all of us will be a beneficiary one day. Anyone who inherits money, property or personal items from parents, grandparents, friends or siblings is a beneficiary. It can be a very confusing role. While you are waiting for your inheritance, you may ask the executor in charge of the estate for information and receive a hostile answer, or perhaps no answer at all. How do you know whether you've stepped over a line that caused a problem? Will asking questions cause family discord? Do you even have a right to ask what you want to ask? Should you hire a lawyer? It can be difficult to navigate through an estate without reliable information.

This book contains the answers to 175 questions asked most by beneficiaries just like you. As a lawyer and estate planner, I've heard these questions from beneficiaries of all ages, in all income brackets, from all types of families, and in all locations. No matter where in Canada we live or how much (or little) we expect to inherit, our situations are similar. Our issues and concerns about estates are the same. We just want to know what to expect, and what to do if our expectations are not met.

The answers you'll find here are based on my experience in a legal career that has spanned almost thirty years so far. This area of law is my passion! When it comes to estates, I've been involved in almost everything. I've drafted thousands of wills. I've contested wills. I've administered estates with modest values and those with multi-millions of dollars. I've chaired committees and given seminars. I've stood in courtrooms and argued over powers of attorney. I've written books and articles, and appeared dozens of times on TV and radio. I've blogged about wills and estates for years.

But most of all, I've listened. I've talked with thousands of parents who are planning wills to look after their children. I've talked with the executors, both the kind who want to do a good job, and the kind who think they've personally won the lottery. I've sat down with families who have lost a parent, and heard the worry and doubt and disappointment, as well as the joy and gratitude of being a beneficiary. I've taken calls from listeners on radio shows, read countless email questions, and received hundreds of questions on my blog.

I want to share what I've learned in plain, readable English with those who need information.

The information in this book is broken down into general topics to help you find the specific answer you're looking for. These general topics range from tax to executor's duties and everything in between. This book is also easy to browse through if you just want to know more about beneficiaries' rights in general. The questions and answers are bite-sized and easy to work with, though some contain more lengthy explanations than others.

I have made every effort to check and double-check the facts relied on when giving my answers. Please remember that laws change constantly, and it's always a good idea to consult a local lawyer with your question to make sure you have the most up-to-date information.

Please remember that the information offered here is necessarily general. It could never replace a one-on-one conversation with an experienced lawyer who can sit down with you in person and hear the full details of your situation. What you read here is information, not legal advice. Use the information you find here as the starting point for your enquiries.

Chapter 1: The Will

This chapter contains questions and answers about the will document itself. The executor of an estate will take the will to a lawyer, but the beneficiaries rarely get any information about the will unless there is a major problem. Here, we will cover witnessing, legal language used in the will, as well as many other topics.

1. Why won't the executor show me the will?

This is the question that beneficiaries ask more often than any other, so it is deserving of being the first question answered in this book.

A will is a private document that belongs to the deceased person. Part of the executor's job is to protect that person's privacy. Just as you don't show your bank statements, pay stubs and car loan details to anyone who asks, neither does the executor show a deceased person's private documents to anyone who asks. If you are a residuary beneficiary of the estate, you are entitled to see the full will after the testator (the person whose will it is) has died. If you're not a residuary beneficiary, the executor is well within his rights to refuse to show you the will.

This question is usually asked by a child or other family member of the person who has passed away. Though you may not like it, the fact that you are a family member of the deceased does not mean you can see the will.

2. Who is a residuary beneficiary?

A residuary beneficiary is any person or charity who is supposed to inherit some or all of the residue of an estate.

The residue of an estate is the portion of the estate that remains once all of the bills and taxes have been paid, and after specific gifts such as a piece of jewelry or a specified sum of money, have been paid. Normally it's pretty easy to spot the residuary beneficiaries in a will. Look for language such as "I divide my estate equally between my children", or "I leave my estate to my spouse". Those references to the estate are actually references to the *residue*, because they mean to leave the full estate to the beneficiaries after bills, taxes and specific gifts are paid.

3. Why can a residuary beneficiary see the will when other beneficiaries cannot?

Some beneficiaries are supposed to receive something specific, such as a piece of jewelry, the proceeds of a certain account, or a set sum of money. These gifts, in most cases, don't really depend on the rest of the estate. For example, the set sum of money is going to be the same amount whether the estate contains $500 or $500,000, unless of course the estate is insolvent. Therefore, there is no need for the person receiving an item like this to know more about the estate. He only needs to know about the gift going to him. In other words, a beneficiary who is not a residuary beneficiary is treated on a "need to know" basis.

On the other hand, a residuary beneficiary is by definition receiving "the rest of" an estate. He couldn't possibly know what "the rest" is if he doesn't know what's in the estate, what the bills are, and what the taxes are likely to be. Therefore, a residuary beneficiary is entitled to see the will, as well as all documentation used for probate purposes, including an inventory of the estate.

Being a residuary beneficiary also carries legal rights and obligations. The residuary beneficiaries are the people who police the executor to make sure that he or she is doing the job properly. They can't do that if they don't know what's in the estate and what the will says.

4. Who gets to see the will while our parents are still alive?

Nobody has a right to see your parents' wills except for your parents. They may choose to tell you what's in it, or even to show it to you, but you have no legal right to insist on it. And why would you want to see their wills anyway if they are not looking for your input? Most of the time, even an executor normally doesn't see what's in a will until the testator has passed away, as the executor has no right to insist on seeing the will while the person is still alive.

If someone is acting under an Enduring Power of Attorney (also known as Power of Attorney for Property, Continuing Power of Attorney or Durable Power of Attorney), for your parent, that person has a right to see and safely store the parent's will. Note this only applies once the Power of Attorney <u>has been properly activated</u> and the person has stepped into the decision-making role for your parent. You don't have a right to see your parents' wills just because your name is on a Power of Attorney document that has never been used.

5. Who can see the will after our parents have passed away?

The person named as executor has the right not just to see the will, but to take possession of it. He will read the will to see who the beneficiaries are, and should give a copy of the will to the residuary beneficiaries at some point during his administration of the estate. Although people find it very hard to accept this, the fact that you were related to someone – even closely related – gives you no legal right to see their will.

6. The executor says I'm not a residuary beneficiary, but I don't believe him. What can I do?

If you find that you cannot accept the executor's word that you are not a beneficiary of an estate that he or she is administering, then you need to get this information in writing. The most effective way to do this is to hire a lawyer to write a letter to the executor or the lawyer who is acting for the estate and ask for written confirmation that you are not a beneficiary. If you receive this confirmation and the executor is lying about it, you have the paperwork you need to sue him.

If you receive a letter from the estate lawyer that says you are not a beneficiary, you can believe it. No lawyer is going to risk his or her license to practice law just to make sure you don't get a peek at a will you're entitled to see.

7. Are hand-written wills valid?

Hand-written (or "holographic") wills are valid in some provinces in Canada and not in others. The provinces which allow hand-written wills at the time this guide was prepared are: Alberta, Manitoba, New Brunswick, Newfoundland and Labrador, Ontario, Quebec, and Saskatchewan.

A holographic will must be dated and signed by the deceased, but does not need witnesses in order to be valid.

Holographic wills are valid if they are made properly, and the rules around what kind of document qualifies as a holographic will are simple, but one rule in particular is widely broken, with the result that wills end up being invalid. The rule that is generally broken is the one about the document actually being hand-written. According to law, a holographic will is 100% in the handwriting of the deceased. This means that forms in which the deceased simply filled in some blanks, or something that was created on the deceased's computer the printed and signed, do not qualify as proper holographic wills.

Don't be surprised if the executor has told you the holographic will may be problematic, as most of the time they are a bigger mess than the person who wrote it could possibly imagine. It's pretty common that someone prepares a home-made will without regard to the rules of wills, leaving a document that may or may not qualify as a real will. This is because people do not read the instructions properly, omit instructions they don't understand, and mistakenly decide that certain rules don't apply to them.

Sometimes banks and insurance companies won't accept a holographic will unless it has been probated first because they are so frequently problematic. When a will goes through the probate process, the court confirms that the will is valid, which protects the bank or insurance company if they pay out funds from the estate as directed by the will. When a bank or insurance company won't accept an unprobated holographic will, the executor may end up getting a second legal opinion on the validity of the will, or sending the will to the court for the judge to decide if it's valid.

8. What happens if I witnessed the will?

If you were a witness to a will in which you were named a beneficiary, you are no longer a beneficiary. You are not going to get what the will left to you. The will itself is valid, but the gift to you is not, so everyone else will still get their shares. The share of the estate that you would have received if you hadn't witnessed the will is going to be distributed as if there were no will. The same rule applies if the witness was your spouse or common law spouse.

9. What if the lawyer witnessed the will?

This is perfectly alright. In fact, it's normal that the lawyer who prepared the will acts as a witness, with someone from the lawyer's staff acting as the second witness. It's also fine if the same lawyer later acts as lawyer for the estate.

10. What if the executor witnessed the will?

This doesn't invalidate the will. It's not the best idea though, since an executor who witnesses a will may not be able to collect executor's compensation.

11. What if the executor can only find a copy of the will and not the original?

The rules of probate all across Canada say that the original will is required for probate. This is because if an original will can't be found, the law presumes that the testator destroyed the original with the intention of revoking it. In some limited circumstances, a judge will allow a copy of the will to be submitted for probate, but that is unusual. If the executor only has a copy, he or she should take it to an experienced wills lawyer to see if there is anything that can be done.

If the original can't be found, and the executor can't convince a judge that the copy is the last will and testament, the estate will be distributed as if there is no will. This may well change what you are entitled to receive as a beneficiary.

12. What is the affidavit of execution?

In order for a will to be valid, it has to be signed and witnessed properly. Since the deceased will not be around at the key time to vouch for the proper signing of the document, another method had to be devised. That other method is the affidavit of execution. Its name varies from province to province, as it may be called the Affidavit of Witness, or the Proof of Will. In all cases though, it's a document attached to the original will, signed by one of the witnesses who saw the will signed, and sworn before a Commissioner for Oaths or Notary Public. It gives the evidence that all the necessary steps were followed. Generally only one of the witnesses needs to sign one of these.

13. What if Mom didn't know what she was doing when she signed the will?

The law says that a person must have mental capacity to sign a will. If they sign a will without that capacity, the will isn't valid.

This is a really tricky area of law. Sometimes family members will assume that an older parent "didn't know what she was doing" simply because that parent sometimes wasn't as sharp as he or she used to be when younger. Likely the parent showed signs of dementia or Alzheimer's disease or memory loss. It's tough to say whether the parent's issues were so severe as to mean the parent could not sign a will on any given day.

Despite the fact that this is an ugly, heart-breaking kind of lawsuit, and despite the need to bring medical, legal and personal evidence, people do like to rely on this as a catch-all reason to contest a will.

This is not to say that there are no real cases where a will was made by an individual who lacked mental capacity. Certainly there are.

14. What if the will was changed right before my Mom died?

There is nothing unusual about a person on his or her deathbed wanting to write a new will. That happens every day. However, when the will is changed drastically from the previous will, or it is changed with a great deal of secrecy, or if it suddenly leaves out a "logical beneficiary" such as a child, this could be problematic.

The circumstances will be important. If one person stands to benefit greatly from the change, it's important for family members to look at the situation. Is there any logical reason (from the parent's point of view – you don't have to agree with it) for that person to receive an unusual benefit? Was that person present when the new will was signed? Did it appear that this person had an unusual amount of influence over your parent immediately prior to the parent's passing? Was your parent under the influence of medications at the time the will was signed?

If you believe that your parent made a new will under pressure from someone, or that the new will was made when your parent really had no understanding of what was happening, you may be in a position to contest the will. You will likely have legal standing to contest the will if you are a person who was a beneficiary under the old will, or a person who would be a beneficiary if there was no will, such as a child of the deceased.

You could see a lawyer to talk about how to proceed. Be prepared to hear that the lawsuit will be long, expensive, difficult and ugly.

15. What if the executor named in the will has died or won't act?

If the first executor named in the will can't or won't take on the executor role, the alternate named executor has the right to take over as executor. Note, however, that an executor can't quit in the middle of an estate without a judge's permission and a passing of accounts.

If there is a valid will but nobody to act as executor, someone else should put the will through probate with an explanation as to what happened to the named executor. Each province and territory has rules that set out a priority list to say who is in line to take on this job in the absence of a named executor. In most places, a residuary beneficiary under the will ranks higher on that list than some family members.

16. Does the lawyer have to tell me if my parent made a new will removing me as a beneficiary?

No. Anyone who hires a lawyer to help them, whether it's for a new will or any other legal matter, is entitled to confidentiality from the lawyer. Besides, why would the lawyer think it was your business?

17. Isn't there supposed to be a reading of the will?

No. The reading of the will is not a legal requirement. In fact, it's no longer even a custom and is almost never done.

18. The will is 25 years old. Is that ok?

Wills don't expire. As long as a will was valid when it was signed, it will still be valid 25 years later. Unfortunately, the law changes constantly so a will that old will likely be out of date in terms of the law. Also, the deceased person's life probably changed significantly during that 25 years as well, so the will might no longer reflect the deceased's financial or family situation.

19. Mom had early signs of dementia when she signed her will. Does that invalidate the will?

It might invalidate the will, but not necessarily so. A person with the early signs of dementia still has the right to sign a will, as long as that person has the mental capacity to understand the proceedings both on the day the instructions were given to the lawyer, and on the day the will was signed.

20. I'm married now so my surname is different from the will. Am I still going to get my inheritance?

Yes, there is an easy administrative fix for this situation. If the will describes you using your maiden name, the application for probate should describe you using both the maiden name and the married name to show that you are one person. For example, if your maiden name was Susan Wong and your married name is Susan James, the probate application should call you "Susan James, in the will written as Susan Wong".

21. What if there's more than one will?

The most recent will is the will that must be sent to the court for probate. As a general rule, the first sentence of a new will revokes any previous wills. Even if the will is not going to be probated, the most recent will is the one that is valid. An exception to this can happen in Ontario, where multiple wills are currently allowed. The wording of the wills must make it clear that they are intended to co-exist and that one does not revoke the other.

There could also be more than one will if the deceased owned property in another jurisdiction. This normally means in another country. Again, the wording of the wills must specifically make it clear that the wills are intended to co-exist without revoking each other.

22. Are wills made from will kits valid?

Will kit wills can be valid. They have to be properly signed, dated and witnessed just like any other will. They are not considered by law to be handwritten wills, so they must have two witnesses. Whether they are properly structured or contain legally valid instructions is another matter. Hopefully an executor who is faced with a will kit will is going to take it to a lawyer for an opinion on whether it's valid.

Chapter 2: Probate

The executor of the estate may have told you that he or she is applying to the court to probate the will that names you as a beneficiary. If you're like most beneficiaries, that information is valuable, but not helpful, as you won't really know what is involved. This chapter should help shed some light on the process, cost and meaning of probate.

23.　What is probate?

Probate is a court process that confirms that a will is the valid last will of a deceased person, confirms the appointment of the executor, and confirms the distribution as set out in the will. The executor named in the will submits a detailed package of information to the court to be reviewed by a judge. The package of information includes the original will, evidence about the signing of the will, an inventory of the estate, and information about the family and other beneficiaries.

Getting probate doesn't usually require anyone to appear personally in front of a judge. The executor (or, more likely, his lawyer) might have to appear in person if the judge has questions about the probate documents, or if there is some kind of rush to get the probate more quickly.

Having a will probated protects everyone involved in the estate, including the beneficiaries.

24. What information about me, the beneficiary, is included in an application for probate?

Your full name, address, age and relationship to the deceased person will be included, as will a description of what you are supposed to inherit under the will. If you are mentally or physically handicapped, that will also be stated in the application for probate.

25. Does every will have to go through probate?

No. Whether or not a will has to go through probate usually depends on the type of asset the deceased person owned, and the value of those assets. Certain assets, such as real estate that is held only in the name of the deceased, will always require probate. Bank accounts and investment accounts almost always require probate as well, but if they are small accounts, the bank may be willing to release them without the need for going through probate.

There could also be other reasons why an executor must get probate. If there is any question about the validity of the will, such as improper witnessing, probate will be required. This could also be the case if parts of the will are contradictory or unclear. If there are disputes brewing between family members, the executor may want to get probat that he can get the protection of the court

28. What does probate cost?

Each province and territory in Canada sets its own probate fee, which is a fee paid to the court at the time the court processes a will or codicil for probate. The fee is charged against the estate as it is shown on the inventory that forms part of the application for probate. The following chart shows the fees payable at the time of publication of this manual:

Alberta	$25 for estates under $10,000
	$100 for estates between $10,000 and $24,999
	$200 for estates between $25,000 and $124,999
	$300 for estates between $125,000 and $249,999
	$400 for estates of $250,000 or more
British Columbia	$0 for estates under $10,000
	$208 for estates between $10,001 and $25,000
	$6 for every $1,000 (or part of $1,000) by which the value of the estate exceeds $25,000 but is not more than $50,000
	Plus $14 for every $1,000 (or part of $1,000) by which the value of the estate exceeds $50,000
Manitoba	$50 for the first $10,000
	$6 for every $1,000 by which the value of the estate exceeds $10,000

New Brunswick	$5 for each $1,000
Newfoundland and Labrador	$85 for the first $10,000
	$5 for every $1,000 by which the value of the estate exceeds $10,000
	Plus $50 for the probate Order
Northwest Territories	$25 for estates under $10,000
	$100 for estates between $10,000 and $25,000
	$200 for estates between $25,000 and $125,000
	$300 for estates between $125,000 and $250,000
	$400 for estates worth $250,000 or more
Nova Scotia	$70 for estates under $10,000
	$176 for estates between $10,000 and $25,000
	$293 for estates between $25,000 and $50,000
	$820 for estates between $50,000 and $100,000
	Plus $13.85 for each $1,000 (or part of $1,000) by which the value of the estate exceeds $100,000
Nunavut	$25 for estates under $10,000
	$100 for estates between $10,000 and $25,000
	$200 for estates between $25,000 and $125,000
	$300 for estates between $125,000 and $250,000
	$400 for estates worth $250,000

	or more
Ontario	$5 for each $1,000 for the first $50,000
	Plus $15 for each $1,000 (or part of $1,000) by which the value of the estate exceeds $50,000
Prince Edward Island	$50 for estates up to 10,000
	$400 for estates from $10,001 to $100,000
	Plus $4 for each $1,000 (or part of $1,000) by which the value of the estate exceeds $100,000
	Plus closing fee of 0.2%
Quebec	$0 for notarial wills
	$65 for non-notarial wills
Saskatchewan	$7 for every $1,000 (or part of $1,000) of estate value
Yukon	$0 for estates up to $25,000
	$140 for estates that exceed $25,000

29. Does the estate need a lawyer to go through probate?

Not always, though most executors are glad of the help. There are a lot of forms to fill in and hoops to jump through to get probate, and many executors don't want to take chances on dealing with all that legal process on their own. Also, in some parts of Canada, wills are still written in archaic legal language which can trip up an executor who doesn't really know what that language means. However, there is no law that says that an application for probate must be prepared by a lawyer.

The main role of a lawyer for an estate is to advise the executor about what needs to be done legally, but some executors choose not to look for this advice.

30. Where does the executor get the values he puts on the inventory?

Many beneficiaries take issue with the values placed on assets during the probate process. Some think the executor is putting too high a value on items, but the majority believes that the executor is under-valuing things. The inventory prepared by the executor is part of a sworn affidavit, so the executor is aware that he or she is swearing under oath that the values are accurate. Very few beneficiaries are as good at valuing property as they think they are, and constant second-guessing of the executor's valuations often leads to disputes.

The best approach for a beneficiary to take is not to insist that you know the value best, but simply to insist that the executor get appraisals or statements to back up the values he or she is using. You may think you know the value of your parents' house, for example, but if the executor hires a professional, independent appraiser whose opinion is different from yours, you may just have to accept that that person knows more about it than you do.

Generally speaking, the executor's accounting is presented to the beneficiaries without appraisals, receipts, correspondence or other original paperwork attached, as the accounting is intended to summarize the executor's actions. However, if you really do think that the executor is way off track on the value of a specific asset, it is alright to ask to see whatever appraisal or other paperwork the executor is using.

Executors should take values for real property, including homes, vacation properties, rental properties, raw land, and commercial properties either from an appraisal made by a registered, qualified land appraiser or a current municipal tax certificate.

Values of monetary assets should be taken from current bank or investment statements. Values of private companies should be determined by the company's accountant. All assets such as paintings, collections, antiques, vehicles, boats, jewelry, etc. should be appraised.

Beneficiaries should be aware that the values that are shown on the inventory are date of death values. When a person dies on September 1st but the inventory of his estate is not prepared until October 30, the inventory will give a snapshot of the financial situation on September 1st. Don't be upset or suspicious if you see, for example, a credit card debt on the inventory of your mother's estate even though you know that credit card was paid off after your mother's death.

31. The bank says we don't need probate if we all sign a form. What's that all about?

In some cases, a bank will agree to release a bank account to an executor without going through probate. This is rare, and only applies where the account in question is the only asset in the estate and is pretty small. The idea behind it is that it helps the estate save costs and time by not requiring the executor to go through the probate process. This isn't something that an executor has a legal right to demand, but may find out is available if the bank agrees.

If the bank agrees, there is an indemnity form that all beneficiaries of the estate must sign before the account is released. It replaces the legal protection offered by the probate. By signing the form, you are agreeing that the bank may release the deceased's funds to the executor, and you can't take it back later if you change your mind.

This is a pretty common practice across Canada and if you are the beneficiary of a small estate, you just may run into it.

32. Is it true that you don't have to probate wills in Quebec?

Yes and no. This is only true if the will in question is a notarial will. This means a will that was prepared by a Quebec notary and signed in front of the notary. If the will is a holographic will, or some other non-notarial will, you may have to go through probate. The legal system with respect to will is much different in Quebec than any other province or territory.

Chapter 3: Funeral Arrangements

This is a very short chapter, but in my view, very important. One of the most difficult aspects of being a beneficiary is that you've recently lost someone who is dear to you. Being excluded from decisions regarding funeral, burial or cremation can be painful, so I hope this chapter brings some useful information about the process and explains why you might not be consulted.

33. Who has the legal right to decide about burial or cremation?

It's up to the executor of the estate to decide how to deal with the deceased's remains. This means all decisions about burial, cremation, ceremonies, flowers, officiating and the other details that go into this important event. Even if the executor is not the next of kin, by law the executor still gets to choose what is done. This could mean, for example, that a man appoints his friend to be his executor, so his friend could get to decide the funeral arrangements rather than the deceased man's widow.

You as a beneficiary do not have any right to decide anything about the funeral, with one exception. If you believe that the executor has badly over-spent on the funeral arrangements, at the time of the final accounting you may object to this aspect. Other than that, you must accept that the deceased chose his or her executor, and thereby chose the person who would make the funeral arrangements.

34. If there are funeral instructions in the will, doesn't everyone have to follow them?

No. Any funeral or cremation instructions that the deceased included in his will are considered in law to be an expression of wishes only. It's not legally binding on anyone. Usually though, an executor will take an expression of wishes into consideration if possible.

35. What if I don't agree with the funeral arrangements that are being made?

If you as a beneficiary don't agree with funeral arrangements, you may of course voice your objections, but you have no right in law to insist on any particular arrangements. When it is a family member who has passed away and there are different ideas about funeral arrangements being talked about, it's a good idea to suggest that the executor and the immediate family sit down together to talk about what is to be done. That way, everyone at least gets to have their say.

36. How much is the executor allowed to spend on the funeral?

There is no guideline or rule that sets out a specific dollar amount for a funeral. However, there is a lot of case law in Canada that says an executor should spend a "reasonable" amount based on the deceased's station in life, and the estate's ability to pay. It wouldn't make sense, for example, for an estate of only $15,000 to be depleted by a $12,000 funeral. It also wouldn't make a lot of sense for a millionaire's family to spend only $3,000 on a funeral. Every case has to be decided on its own facts.

37. Can I get reimbursed for the cost of flying to another city to attend the funeral?

No. Each beneficiary and each family member must pay his or her own transportation to and from the funeral, as well as any hotel stays or meals purchased to attend a funeral. Often beneficiaries will ask the executor to advance them some money against their share so that they can attend the funeral, but this doesn't usually work because the executor likely won't have access to any of the deceased's assets at that early stage.

Chapter 4: Joint Property

One of the most confusing aspects of an estate is dealing with joint property. The initial source of the problem is that the people who own the asset frequently misunderstand the legal rights of other owners. This may be compounded by an executor who is similarly confused. This chapter is intended to increase your familiarity with the meaning of joint property. I also hope to inform you about what steps need to be taken, either by the executor or by you, once the other joint owner of an asset has died, leaving the asset in your name.

38.   Is joint property included in an estate?

As a general rule, any property that is jointly owned with a right of survivorship is not included in an estate. Note that the word "property" in estate law doesn't just mean real estate. It means everything that a person owns. *Real property* is real estate, including land, buildings, mineral titles, homes, cabins, and rental properties. *Personal property* means everything that isn't real estate, and includes bank accounts, investments, household items, vehicles, boats, music collections, receivables, digital assets, shares of companies, etc.

The exception to the rule is that where property of any kind is jointly owned in an inter-generational arrangement and the older person passes away, the property IS part of the estate. This situation usually involves a parent and child, but could be an aunt/uncle and their niece/nephew, or could be a grandparent/grandchild. See question 39 for more on this.

Joint property is not the same as tenants-in-common, even though both legal arrangements have two or more names on one title. See question 39 below for more on this. You would have to get an updated title search from the land titles registry to find out which arrangement is in place.

39. What if an asset was only put into joint names by the deceased for convenience?

Often a parent adds one or more of his or her children to the parent's asset as joint owners. Nothing causes more havoc in an estate! The problem is that where an asset is jointly owned, there is an assumption by the younger owner of the asset that joint ownership conveys the usual right of survivorship, or in other words, the child will own the asset when the parent dies. But if the parent has only put the child's name on the asset so that the child could help with the banking, or to avoid probate fees, there is a question in law about whether the parent ever intended the child to actually own the asset. It's pretty difficult to prove what a parent intended, as each joint owner child says he or she was supposed to own the asset, and every other beneficiary says they were not.

This leads to confusion, fighting and accusations of taking advantage of the aging parent.

The exception to the rule about not including joint property in an estate applies where:
- The asset originally belonged to a parent; AND
- The parent added a child, niece or nephew as a joint owner of the asset; AND
- There is no written confirmation by the parent made at the time the asset was made joint to the effect that the parent intended to give ownership of the asset.
- Where this situation exists and the parent passes away, the joint asset DOES become part of the parent's estate.

40. If our Mom left her house to all of us kids jointly, what are the issues?

A huge number of parents leave the family home equally among their children, and in the vast majority of cases, this turns out to be a big mistake. Two, three, or more names are added to one house as joint owners. The issues vary from family to family, of course, but there are certain questions that commonly lead to disputes. Who gets to live there if they all own it? What if the home needs a new roof but the children who don't use the house refuse to chip in? Who pays the property tax and the fire insurance? What if one child rents out the house to a tenant without the permission of the others and won't share the revenue? All of this and more happens on a regular basis.

Assuming at least one of the children owns his or her own home, adding that child's name to the title of another property only ends up creating a tax problem for that child. The child will incur capital gains tax when the house is sold.

Added to all of this is the difficulty of selling the property. Assuming the children get fed up with trying to deal with the impossible sharing of title and want to sell, they then all have to agree on the timing, the price, the choice of realtor and more. This is generally impossible for a group of siblings to achieve and often takes a lawsuit to settle the sale.

Parents who take this step are simply refusing to do any real planning, and leaving the issues for the kids to figure out. Perhaps a good route for a beneficiary to go is to suggest that the group get together as soon as possible after the parent's death, talk about who really wants the house and who does not, and figure out a way for the one who wants it to buy out the others.

Another idea is to sell the house right off before it is even put into the beneficiaries' names, and split the money between you.

41. Can the executor sell the deceased's part of a jointly owned property?

No. If the property is jointly owned by the deceased and another person, the title will belong in law to that other person, and there is nothing for the executor to sell.

42. What's the difference between joint tenants and tenants in common?

The difference for a beneficiary is huge. When two people own a property as joint tenants with right of survivorship, there are no halves or other portions of the property. Each owner owns the entire property. One cannot sell his or her title, and can't leave it to anyone in his or her will if the other owner is alive. When one joint owner dies, the surviving owner gets to keep the entire property. Probate is not required and the property is not part of the estate.

Joint ownership is a "last man standing" arrangement. Only the last surviving owner has anything to leave to his or her beneficiaries.

On the other hand, when two people own a property as tenants in common, each of them owns a pre-determined portion of the property. It could be halves, or any other combination. Either of them could sell his or her share, and can direct where the share is to go using his or her will. Probate is required to transfer the property after death, and the property is part of the estate.

As a beneficiary, you should be aware that "having two names on the title" does NOT always mean joint ownership. If you think you have joint ownership of a property that is listed in the estate, you should consult a lawyer who will get an up-to-date title search and advise you as to what you own or don't own.

43. If I'm a surviving joint tenant, do I have to do anything to get the property?

Yes. If you held a title to a property jointly with someone who passed away, you don't need to go through probate. You do, however, have to go to the land titles office or registry to have the deceased person's name taken off the title. This will NOT happen automatically and you are the person who is responsible for making it happen. You should take a copy of the death certificate and your own identification to the land titles office, where you will be asked to sign and swear some paperwork that will be filed to change the title. There should be no charge, or only a nominal charge, for this change.

If you don't do anything, the deceased person's name stays on the title. You won't be able to sell it, because you won't be able to obtain the signature of the other (deceased) owner. If it is not changed while you're alive, both your will and the deceased person's will would later have to be probated to change the title.

44. What if the will gives me a house that the deceased owned in joint tenancy with someone else?

It does occasionally happen that someone makes a will that tries to give away property that is actually held in a joint tenancy. It happens quite a lot with home-made wills, as the person making the will doesn't really understand what he or she has to give away. A gift like this under a will is not valid if the other joint owner is still alive. The property is not legally yours if the other joint owner is still alive, and you do not get an equal monetary gift either.

Chapter 5: Beneficiary Designations

Being designated as the beneficiary of an asset may be complicated if you don't know exactly what you are entitled to receive. It may also feel strange that the executor won't help you. This chapter should shed some light on your position and what you have to do to collect the asset.

45. What is a beneficiary designation?

A beneficiary designation is a legal way for the owner of an asset to name the person or people who should be given the asset when the owner dies. It is only available for a few specific types of assets.

Most of the time, the reason an owner names a beneficiary this way is that he wants to ensure that the right person receives the asset. There can also be tax benefits for certain designations. For example, a husband who names his wife (or vice versa) as the beneficiary of his RRSP is taking advantage of a tax break that isn't available if he names his children or siblings as the beneficiary of the very same asset.

46. What kinds of assets have beneficiary designations?

The most common assets that carry beneficiary designations are Registered Retirement Savings Plans (RRSPs), Registered Retirement Income Funds (RRIFs), Tax Free Savings Accounts (TFSAs), public and private pensions, Locked in Retirement Accounts (LIRAs), segregated funds and insurance policies. Regular non-registered bank accounts and investment accounts, bonds and term deposits do not have designated beneficiaries.

Registered Educational Savings Plans (RESPs) also carry beneficiary designations but are treated quite differently than other instruments. See question 49 for more about RESPs.

47. If my Mom left me an insurance policy, is that in the estate?

If you are the named beneficiary of an insurance policy or any other asset, that asset does not become part of the deceased's estate. It is not included in the assets controlled by the will. The policy should not be listed in the estate inventory and should not be added in for the purpose of calculating the probate fee. The funds are paid directly to you by the insurance company and do not pass through the hands of the executor.

This means that the executor is not responsible for making sure that you get your policy. You are responsible for that yourself. The executor's job is simply to provide you with a copy of the death certificate together with the policy number (if he knows it), so that you can contact the insurance company.

48. If my Mom leaves me an insurance policy, does that mean I get less from the estate?

Confusion sometimes arises when a parent makes a will that says the estate is to be divided equally among the children, but then also leaves an insurance policy to one of the kids. It may seem to the other children that it isn't fair for one child to get "more" when the will talks about an equal division. However, the will only deals with what is in the estate, and as mentioned, the proceeds of a life insurance policy are not part of the estate. There is no legal reason why a parent cannot leave both a policy and an equal share of the estate to one of the children.

49. My mom had an RESP for my child, but now the executor says there is no RESP. What's up with that?

RESPs can be a problem in many estates. The confusion arises because the people who own them think they work like RRSPs, but they do not work like that.

The person who set up the RESP (the parent or grandparent) is the owner of the RESP plan. If the paperwork that set up the RESP named an alternate owner, on the death of the original owner the plan will pass to that new owner, who will carry on with the plan as before. Eventually the child would receive the funds, assuming the child attended post-secondary education.

However, most plan owners don't realize they have to name an alternate owner of the plan. This is where the problem arises. If they pass away without naming an alternate owner, the RESP collapses when the owner dies. The money in the plan becomes part of the estate and the matching grants received from the government must be returned to the government. The child who was named under the RESP would get nothing.

Collapsing of the plan can also be avoided if the will is used to name an alternate owner of the plan.

50. The executor says he isn't going to do the paperwork for the RRSP that I'm inheriting. Isn't he supposed to do that?

No. The executor's job is to deal with and distribute the assets in the estate. An RRSP isn't in the estate. The executor's job would be to advise you of the RRSP that names you (assuming he knows about it), and to provide you with a copy of the death certificate. The executor should also let the bank know that the owner has passed away. It's then up to you to go to the bank with your identification and the death certificate and request that the RRSP be paid to you.

If the deceased leaves you an RRSP or RRIF, you are entitled to receive the full amount in the account. Any tax on the RRSP or RRIF comes out of the estate (unless you are the spouse of the deceased and the RRSP/RRIF is rolled over to you), and that paperwork is for the executor to do.

51. What is a "rollover"?

"Rollover" is a tax term. It refers to an arrangement whereby an asset that would normally be taxed when the owner dies can be transferred to another person without the tax being payable. It delays the payment of the taxes until the person who receives the asset also passes away, or sells the asset.

Rollovers are available only in limited situations. One of the most common rollover situations is that of a deceased spouse's RRSP or RRIF being transferred to a surviving spouse. For example, if Alfred owns a RRIF when he dies, the law says that the RRIF was cashed out a minute before Alfred dies. This means the whole RRIF is now taxable and Alfred's estate must pay the tax before Alfred's beneficiaries can receive anything. However, Alfred may have named his wife, Alice, as the designated beneficiary. If so, the entire RRIF can be rolled over to Alice with no tax being payable at the time. The tax is only paid on money that Alice takes out of the RRIF, or on whatever is left when Alice passes away.

Alfred would not be able to roll the RRIF to his children or anyone else (with the exception that there is a rollover available to a disabled child).

A rollover is also available for farm properties that are being passed from one generation of the family to another. Without the rollover, there would be enormous tax liability arising from the passing of so much land to beneficiaries, and that would destroy most farms.

52. If the designated beneficiary is no longer alive, who gets the asset?

The general rule is that if a policy or plan names a beneficiary who died before the owner of the asset, the asset becomes part of the owner's estate. For example, if Tom names Mary as the beneficiary of his RRIF but Mary died, then when Tom dies his RRIF will become part of his estate. The RRIF would then be distributed according to Tom's will.

53. What if two beneficiaries are named but only one is still alive?

Wording is always important on any specific document. Assuming that a policy or plan names two (or more) beneficiaries using words such as "equally among them", then the surviving beneficiary should receive the entire proceeds. For example, if Tom might leave an insurance policy "equally to my brothers, Robert and Don".

However, if at the time Tom passes away, Robert is already deceased, then Don will receive the full proceeds of the policy.

If the beneficiary designation is set up so that Robert gets 25%, Don gets 25% and Doug gets 50%, things would operate differently. If Doug had already passed away, his share would fall into Tom's estate, and Robert and Don would each still get their 25%.

54. Can the executor change the beneficiary designation?

No. The executor has no control at all over assets with designated beneficiaries. If an asset like this falls into the estate, the executor must treat it as part of the residue of the estate. Note that someone acting under a Power of Attorney cannot change beneficiary designations either. If an investment that is held in an RRSP or RRIF needs to be renewed while the Power of Attorney is in effect, he or she is legally obligated to continue the designation that was originally attached to that RRSP or RRIF.

Chapter 6: Your Rights as a Beneficiary

In almost every estate I've ever worked on, beneficiaries are suspicious of the executor and of the estate lawyer, and of the estate administration process in general. I believe that much of the suspicion and distrust arise out of the fact that nobody is telling the beneficiaries much of anything, least of all what they have a right to expect from the executor and the estate process. This chapter contains answers to a variety of questions that beneficiaries ask me when they feel completely lost.

55. What if the item or money left to me in the will is no longer there when the deceased died?

Normally this would mean that you are out of luck and there is nothing for you to inherit. You can't sue to get it, as it was a gift and not a contract. If, however, the item existed at the time of the death but has disappeared since the death, that's another story. If the item went missing while the executor was in charge, the executor is responsible for making sure you get that gift, even if it means paying for it himself or herself.

56. How do I know whether I'm a beneficiary?

Generally speaking, you won't know until either you see the will, or the executor tells you that you are named in the will. You will receive notice from the executor advising you of what you are supposed to receive.

I'm often told by beneficiaries that they don't trust the executor who tells them they are not beneficiaries of an estate. This is particularly common where the person who passed away was a relative who may have included other family members in the will. If you find that you simply cannot accept the executor's word for it, you might consider hiring a lawyer to write to the executor and request a formal confirmation that you are not a beneficiary.

Another way to find out is to go to the courthouse closest to where the deceased lived and search to see whether the executor has filed for probate. If so, you may request a copy of the probate application. This can't be done immediately following the death, as it's rare that an executor manages to have the application for probate filed within the first couple of months.

57. When do I get a notice?

In jurisdictions in which a notice is required to be sent to a beneficiary, it is normally sent at the time the will is sent to probate. This can be anywhere from a month to three or four months after someone has passed away.

58. Why is the executor making me wait for my inheritance until he has paid all the bills?

That's the law. In every jurisdiction in Canada, debts and bills of the deceased must be paid before any beneficiary receives anything. Some people pass away leaving more debts than assets, in which case their beneficiaries will get nothing, despite what the will might say.

59. What if Dad promised ME that asset?

Most of the time, promises from one person to another to leave them something in the will are not legally enforceable. A person has a right to change his or her mind about what to give someone, after all. But under certain circumstances, a would-be beneficiary can successfully contest the will on the basis of a promise made.

In order for a claim like this to be successful, the deceased must have said or done something to make you believe that you would inherit an asset. Once that is said or done, your believing that it's a real promise must be reasonable. And finally, you must have made decisions or taken action based on that promise, and must have suffered some detriment by relying on the promise. This generally takes the form of someone putting lot of work, time and money into a property or business on the understanding that he would one day inherit it, especially if that person could have done better for himself elsewhere.

If you can't make a good case for yourself based on these principles, you will not be successful with your claim. If your Dad said once about 35 years ago that he might leave you the house and it was never mentioned again and you didn't do anything in particular based on that promise, then your chances are slim to none.

60. Do I have to repay money my parents gave me while they were alive?

The law says that any significant amounts of money that were given or loaned to the children of a deceased person while that person was alive are considered to be advances on the children's inheritance. This means that you would be required to repay the amount that was given or loaned to you.

Even if your parent said to you that you don't have to repay it, you still do. The removal of the requirement to repay it only changes it from a loan to a gift, which is still caught by this law. If you can show by way of paperwork such as bank statements that you repaid the money, then you would not have to repay it.

This may change, depending on the will itself. If the will says specifically that the children do not have to repay any loans, gifts or advancements, then you no longer have to repay it. Unfortunately, most wills don't even address this question.

If you have received funds from your parent during his or her lifetime, and you are supposed to receive an inheritance from his or her estate, the funds you already received can be deducted from your share of the estate. This way, even if you refuse to co-operate with the process, the executor can reduce your share by the amount you already received.

61. What if I don't think the will treats people fairly?

Since it isn't your will or your money, it isn't up to you to decide what's fair.

62. Don't all of us kids have to be treated equally?

No. It is not the law that all children in a family must be treated equally under a will. It is certainly customary in Canada, but it's not a legal requirement. Parents often leave an uneven distribution because they have helped one child more than the others, or because they feel that one child is disadvantaged.

In British Columbia, the law allows a child to contest a parent's will if he or she is not left an equal share, and can show that it is not fair to receive less.

A child who is a minor or a handicapped adult must be left at least an equal share of an estate. Depending on the size of the estate and other circumstances in any particular estate, the minor or handicapped child may receive more than an equal share. This is particularly true where a handicapped child must have enough to live on for his or her whole life.

63. My wife's parents left her an inheritance but my wife passed away before they did. Do I inherit her share?

Not unless the parent's will specifically leaves it to you. The law does not automatically give a wife or husband's inheritance to their spouse. Laws of intestacy will usually give the share to the deceased wife or husband's children. It may be held in trust, depending on the age of the children. If there are no children, it would go back to the parent's estate. If the will says that the share should go to you, those specific instructions will override the general law.

64. The executor says there isn't enough in the estate to give me my inheritance. I know there was some money there at the time of death. How can that be?

Beneficiaries of an estate only get to inherit what is left after bills, expenses and taxes are all paid. Perhaps the deceased died with debt, which could wipe out an inheritance. Perhaps the deceased had not been up to date with income tax returns, and there were back taxes owing. The executor will produce an inventory of all assets and liabilities that existed at the date of death, and will later produce an accounting of what he or she did with estate assets. You should be able to tell from examining the accounting why you will not be receiving your gift, or at least not all of it.

65. What's the residue of an estate?

The residue of an estate is everything that is left in an estate after the following have been paid from the estate:

- Debts such as loans or mortgages;
- Funeral costs;
- Tax owing for the year of death, or for previous years;
- Bills such credit cards, cell phones or utilities used by the deceased;
- Gifts under the will or Memorandum of Personal Effects, such as jewelry;
- Executor's compensation;

- Specific gifts in the will such as a specified sum of money.

66. If I'm receiving provincial disability benefits, will receiving an inheritance bump me off the benefits?

Yes, if the amount of your inheritance causes you to own more money than is allowed by the provincial benefits plan. The provincial plan will have an asset test, and if you own more than the amount allowable, your benefits will be reduced. You could be cut off completely if your inheritance is paid to you in a lump sum.

If the will directs that your inheritance is to be held in a type of trust known as a Henson trust, you will not be cut off from your benefits. This is possible in every province except Alberta, which does not allow Henson trusts.

67. Does the executor have to cash everything in?

No, not unless the will directs him or her to do so, or there is no other way to distribute the assets according to the will. A properly worded will should contain specific authorities for the executor that define how much flexibility he or she will have.

68. My mom had a reverse mortgage. How does that affect her estate, and me as a beneficiary?

A reverse mortgage will be registered against the title of the house. It must be paid out by the estate before the house is sold or transferred to someone else. In some cases, the existence of the reverse mortgage means that the house itself must be sold to pay off the mortgage because there are no other assets to do that. Beneficiaries do not have the right to inherit until and unless all debts of the estate are paid first. This could mean that even if the house was left to you, you won't be able to receive it unless there is enough money in the estate to pay out the reverse mortgage first.

69. I'm a step-child. Am I included in the gift to 'children'?

A gift to "my children" in a will automatically includes biological children, whether those children were born inside or outside of a marriage or common law relationship. "Children" also includes legally adopted children. It does not, however, include step-children, even if those step-children were raised by the deceased like one of his or her own. The only exception would be specific language in the will that specifically says that step-children are included.

70. Can I turn down my inheritance?

Yes. Anyone can refuse an inheritance, as it is a gift. You would have to provide a written, signed, witnessed waiver form to the executor. This doesn't apply if you are in bankruptcy, as your inheritance must by law be paid to the trustee in bankruptcy. The estate lawyer may be willing to draw up a waiver for you to sign.

71. Can I ask that my inheritance go to someone else?

If you have waived your inheritance, you will have no say in where it goes. The estate will proceed as if you were never involved. However, if you have agreed to receive your inheritance, you can sign a form called an Assignment and Direction to Pay, which will instruct the executor to pay some or all of your funds to someone else. This doesn't apply if you are in bankruptcy.

72. Can I inherit if I'm in bankruptcy?

If you are in bankruptcy at the time someone passes away and leaves you assets, those assets must be paid to the trustee in bankruptcy. The trustee may use as much of your inheritance as is needed to pay off your creditors. If there is anything left of your inheritance after that, the trustee will pay that to you.

Sometimes people in bankruptcy try to get around this rule by saying that even though they were in bankruptcy at the time the person died, they didn't actually receive anything until months later. In fact, some try to get the executor to hang on to the inheritance for them until they are discharged from bankruptcy. This is illegal.

73. My husband died and my name is not on our house. Now what do I do?

That depends on where you live, and what it says in the will. If the will leaves you the house, then you will not have to leave your home. You will simply have to take the probate to the Land Titles registry and take care of paperwork that will transfer the house to you.

If there is no will, you will have to rely on the laws of your area. The law varies from province to province in terms of the surviving spouse's rights. In NL, for example, a house that is owned by one spouse only automatically becomes a joint property when the spouse who owns the title passes away. In other places, there is a right to stay in the home for a certain amount of time only, before it is sold.

If there is a will but it doesn't leave the house to you, you may wish to apply to the court for a greater share of the estate so that you can hold onto the house. This is by no means a rubber stamp and you may not achieve what you want, but it is a solution that's available all across Canada.

All of these suggestions should be discussed with a lawyer before you choose any course of action.

74. When are children old enough to inherit?

Children may not inherit anything, or have their names put on real property until they have reached the age of majority.

75. I'm a common law spouse. Don't I have the same rights as a married spouse?

No, not necessarily. If there is a will leaving the estate to you, there should be no problem. In the absence of a will, the answer to this question very much depends on where you and the deceased lived. In some provinces, a common law relationship gives the same inheritance rights as does a marriage. In other provinces, a person in a common law relationship has absolutely zero right to inherit anything from his or her partner, even if the relationship has been in existence for many years. Many a common law spouse has been shocked and horrified to realize that their spouse left them nothing, not even the home they lived in.

The following chart gives a very brief summary of the provincial and territorial laws that are in place in the event that a person in a common law relationship passes away without a will (known as intestacy).

	Does a common law spouse have a right to inherit on intestacy?
Alberta	Yes, if they have lived together for at least 3 years
British Columbia	Yes, if they have lived together for at least 2 years
Manitoba	Yes, if they lived together for at least 3 years or registered their relationship
New Brunswick	No
Newfoundland and Labrador	No
Northwest Territories	Yes, if they have lived together for at least 2 years
Nova Scotia	No, unless there is a Registered Domestic Partnership
Nunavut	Yes, if they have lived together for at least 2 years
Ontario	No
Prince Edward Island	No
Quebec	No
Saskatchewan	Yes, if they have lived together for at least 2 years
Yukon	No

Chapter 7: The Executor

As a beneficiary, you are an important factor in the estate. The other major player is the executor. This is the person who is in charge, for better or worse. The questions I hear most often about executors usually start off with "Can he get away with that?" Though beneficiaries are often surprised to hear just how much authority an executor has, I believe it is better to have that information and know that the executor is acting within his limits. On the flip side, a beneficiary needs to know when an executor is out of bounds and not doing his job correctly.

76. Can the executor change the locks on Mom's house?

Yes. The executor is legally entitled to change the locks on your parents' house if your parents have passed away. In fact, executors are usually advised by the estate lawyer to change the locks to protect the house itself as well as its contents. After all, others may have a key to the house, such as a housekeeper, caregiver, or neighbour.

If anything goes missing from the house and can't be accounted for, the executor is responsible for it. Therefore an executor would be smart to make sure that nothing can disappear.

Most family members don't see anything wrong with taking something "as a memento". They don't realize that unless the item is given under the will, taking a memento is stealing. As a beneficiary, you should not be helping yourself to anything in the house until the executor has given the go-ahead.

77. How long does the executor have to finish the estate?

The general rule of thumb is that an executor has a year to wind up an estate that has no lawsuits or other complications. In reality, most estates take at least 12 to 18 months to complete, especially if the wait for the tax clearance certificate is factored in.

78. Can the executor rent out mom's house?

As a general rule, renting out the deceased's home is permissible, but as always it depends on the circumstances. Sometimes a will gives a right to someone to continue to live in the home, in which case it couldn't be rented to someone else. In other cases the law automatically gives a spouse or common law spouse a right to live in the home for a certain amount of time following the deceased's death. Obviously the executor couldn't rent out the home if it's otherwise legally occupied.

Assuming it's not otherwise legally occupied, the executor does have the right to rent out the home, but the executor remains responsible for damage or loss to the house. The executor must keep fire insurance on the house as well.

Usually homes are not rented out by executors simply because they are not held in the name of the estate for very long. Nor should they be. Unless there is some good reason why the house is being kept in the estate rather than being sold or transferred to the beneficiaries, it should be dealt with as soon as possible.

79. If there are co-executors, who do I listen to?

Hopefully, both of them. Co-executors are legally required to make decisions regarding the estate together, so you should get the same information and instructions from one as you do from the other.

80. How much can an executor charge?

It's important for a residuary beneficiary to know what an executor is going to receive in term of compensation for administering an estate, as the executor's pay comes out of the residue of the estate. There are three ways to determine what an executor may charge for his or her work on the estate.

The first way to determine the amount of compensation is to read the will to see what it says about compensation. If it contains instructions about compensation, that is what the executor will get. A will may state that the executor gets no compensation at all, or that the executor may receive an amount that well exceeds the norm. If so, that is still what the executor may take, as it was directly authorized by the deceased.

As few wills actually address the issue of executor compensation, the second way of determining the amount is the most common. In these cases, the executor calculates an amount based on several factors, including the time spent and the complexity of the estate. The executor may claim both a fee and, over and above that, his out-of-pocket expenses. The fee should be between 1% and 5% of the value of the estate.

The beneficiaries will then see this claim for compensation as part of the executor's final accounting. If the beneficiaries are not happy about the amount, they and the executor will hopefully be able to negotiate an amount that makes both parties happy.

If the beneficiaries and the executor are not able to come to an agreement, they must rely on the third and final method of determining the compensation. This third method is for the executor to pass his accounts with the court and to ask the judge to set the amount of the compensation. The amount set by the court may be greater or smaller than the amount requested by the executor. If the executor hires a lawyer to pass his accounts, the cost comes out of the residue of the estate.

81. What if the executor won't tell me anything?

This is by far the most common complaint that beneficiaries have about executors. In some cases, the executor just doesn't realize that beneficiaries want more detailed, ongoing reports. In other cases, an executor may be overwhelmed by continual requests by beneficiaries for numbers, paperwork and answers.

The best idea is for beneficiaries and the executor to agree on the frequency of contact. Instead of having half a dozen beneficiaries calling, texting and emailing the executor every day to ask whether the house has been sold, when they can come in to pick up their personal belongings, and where Mom's silverware went, the beneficiaries should agree to wait for regular reports from the executor.

Obviously this only works if the executor co-operates. At the beginning of an estate administration, there is a lot of work to be done. Perhaps at that stage, reports should be sent to the beneficiaries once a week. Later, when most of the work is done and the executor's pace is slowed, the reports could come out once a month.

By "report", I don't mean a fancy document. It need only be a brief email, perhaps in point form, that covers what has happened in the estate that week, such as "probate application was filed on Tuesday, lawyer says it will take 3 weeks, I have scheduled cleaners to come to Mom's house on Friday". Though the executor might be reluctant to agree to regular reports, he or she will soon learn the hard way that not reporting will result in a lot more work.

If the executor simply won't agree to scheduled reports, and in fact won't divulge any information at all even when asked, there may be a problem. An executor who has nothing to hide won't hide anything. You may have to hire a lawyer to make a written demand to the executor for certain information. If you are a residuary beneficiary, you are entitled to know what is going on. Perhaps all of the beneficiaries could pool their resources to share the cost of the lawyer.

82. Can a person be an executor and a beneficiary?

Yes. This is not a conflict of interest. In fact, most executors are also beneficiaries because they are family members of the deceased.

83. The executor hasn't put an obituary in the paper. Doesn't he have to do this?

No. It's not the law that an obituary must be published. It's traditionally done to let neighbours and friends know what has happened and to advise of the date and place of the funeral. The executor may choose not to publish an obituary for privacy reasons, or simply because of the cost.

84. What can happen to an executor who isn't doing the job right?

There are several possible outcomes when an executor fails to do his or her job. All of them require the assistance of the courts. Generally, the beneficiaries of an estate are the ones who bring these matters to court to ask the judge to give them some help. Some of the orders that a judge might give, assuming that the beneficiaries have enough evidence to support their claims, are:

- Removing the executor and appointing someone else in his or her place
- Requiring the executor to produce an accounting, or to produce a better accounting than the one already provided
- Imposing deadlines for certain steps to be taken
- Ordering that a distribution of the estate (at least in part) is to take place immediately
- Reducing the amount of fees that an executor may claim, or refusing to allow any fee whatsoever
- Requiring the executor to pay for estate losses out of his or her own pocket
- Requiring the executor to pay legal costs personally

Although it's rare, executors who steal from an estate or defraud the beneficiaries may go to jail. If the executor ignores the orders made by the judge, this is considered contempt of court and, again, this can end up with the executor in jail.

85. What does it mean when a trust company is an executor?

In Canada, a person may name an individual or a trust company as an executor (note that you cannot name a law firm or an accounting firm, but you can name individual lawyers or accountants). Trust companies are also called "corporate executors". Most are owned by large Canadian banks. A trust company does the same work as any individual executor would do, but unlike individuals, trust companies have highly trained staff and are strictly regulated.

Most people who name a trust company as an executor or co-executor do so because:
- they don't have a suitable family member nearby
- their families are blended or otherwise complex
- they are worried that their children might get into disputes if one has to manage the estate
- their estates are complicated
- they want a trustee to handle a long-term trust for a child, grandchild, or handicapped person
- they simply don't want to place the burden of the estate on their children

From time to time I meet beneficiaries who are offended that their parents chose a trust company to look after the estate. The beneficiary feels that the parent didn't trust him or her, or didn't think that he or she would do a good job. That is rarely the case. Parents tend to choose trust companies for very practical reasons that are generally meant to take the burden off the children.

86. If the executor gets executor's insurance, does that mean he knows something is wrong?

No. Executor's insurance is a fairly new product and most beneficiaries will not be familiar with it. These days, when an executor takes on an estate, he or she may choose to buy executor's insurance that will cover the legal expenses and losses to an estate in the event that the executor is sued. This doesn't necessarily mean that something is wrong. The executor might choose this coverage if the estate assets are complex or unclear, or if family members are already grumbling about the estate before the executor even gets started. It could also be that the will itself is poorly worded or unclear.

It could simply be that the executor realizes that acting as an executor is tough, and that he or she has no experience at it. Mistakes happen even to the most well-intentioned executor.

87. Can the executors hire cleaners and repairmen, or should they do that work themselves?

Executors are entitled to hire the help they need to administer an estate. In most estates, the executor will hire a lawyer to do probate, an accountant to prepare tax returns, and a realtor to sell the house. The expenditures should be reasonable and should be directly related to the work that needs to be done on the estate. An executor does not need to buy a car or hire an assistant to look after an estate.

The executor may also hire cleaners to remove unwanted items from the house, as well as clean carpets and generally clean the place up. If the house needs renovations or maintenance, the executor may also hire people to do this work. If the executor hires contractors or cleaners or tradespeople to work on the house, it is on the understanding that the work done is to make the house more marketable or to improve the selling price.

88. Does the executor have to advertise in the newspaper for creditors?

Each executor must decide whether he or she is going to place an advertisement in the paper for creditors or claimants of an estate. It's not required by law that such an advertisement be placed. Executors choose to place the ad when they feel there is some risk that there might be unpaid creditors of the deceased that the executor doesn't know about.

In a case where a deceased was a business person, the executor may want to make sure that all suppliers and customers who are owed money know about the death, and have a chance to collect their money from the estate. There is less risk of an unknown creditor in other cases, such as where the deceased's affairs had been administered by a family member for the last few years, and the family member is therefore familiar with all the deceased's financial matters.

Finding creditors is important because the law says that all legally enforceable debts must be paid before the beneficiaries may receive anything from the estate.

89. Whose job is it to police the executors?

It's up to the residuary beneficiaries to watch over what an executor does with an estate. There is no government agency or public board to do this. The courts will of course assist a beneficiary of an estate, but there has to be a request by a beneficiary first.

The residuary beneficiaries receive a copy of the will and a copy of the documents that are sent to probate. They should rely on those documents to make sure that the executor is doing what the deceased asked him or her to do in the will.

90. If the executor makes a decision I don't like, can I ask the alternate executor instead?

No. The alternate executor has no legal authority whatsoever unless the first-named executor has passed away, or is unable or unwilling to take on the estate. The first-named executor must be out of the picture entirely before the alternate steps in. For example, the alternate does not get to step in if the first-named executor is on vacation, temporarily ill, or simply busy.

Chapter 8: Personal and Household Items

There are more estate disagreements over personal and household items than there are over money. This is because personal goods owned by the deceased carry sentimental and emotional value in addition to any monetary value. Executors are terrible at getting this part of the estate right, so beneficiaries need to be aware of what is supposed to happen.

91. Can the executor give away items to whoever he wants?

No. The executor can only distribute household goods according to the will or according to a memorandum (or list).

The line gets blurred, at times. Many wills direct that a dispute between beneficiaries about household items is to be decided by the executor. In that case the executor does have to exercise his or her discretion and decide who gets the item.

If the will does not say anything at all about personal or household items, all of those items become part of the residue of the estate and must be distributed to the beneficiaries who are to receive the residue of the estate. The executor is NOT entitled to give personal items to anyone who is not named in the will.

92. If I'm a family member, don't I automatically have a right to get something as a memento?

No. You may only receive a memento of the deceased if you are a beneficiary under the will. Remember, as soon as that person passed away, the items in the home became the property of the beneficiaries. You aren't entitled to take other people's property even if you are related to them. Even if you are a beneficiary named under the will, you have to wait until the executor is ready to allow items to be taken from the home.

93. How does the executor decide what to do if two of us want the same item?

In the case of a dispute, the executor's first step should be to see what the will says about it. More and more wills contain instructions for dealing with this situation and an executor is bound by those instructions.

Where a will doesn't contain any specific instructions, the executor will have to come up with some method of decision-making. It can be as simple as flipping a coin, as this gives an equal chance to both beneficiaries.

94. Is it fair that my sister got something with more value than I did?

That depends on what the will says. Although most wills say that the residue of the will must be divided equally among the children, this doesn't always mean that the household items must also be equally divided. In fact, many parents like to deal with personal and household goods separately from the residue for that very reason; they want the children to choose things they want and like without regard for monetary value. In most cases, dollar values aren't assigned.

95. Do we have to wait for probate before dividing up household items?

This will depend somewhat on the terms of the will. If the will deals with personal and household items separately from the residue, and monetary value is not in issue, the executor may have no reason to wait for probate documents.

96. What if things go missing?

Personal and household goods go missing from a deceased's home with frustrating frequency. Most of the time they are taken by family members who want to get their hands on something valuable before another beneficiary gets there first.

The executor is responsible for items in the home. This is why the locks on the house should be changed and nobody should be allowed in without the executor present. If something has disappeared, the executor should make every effort to find out who took it. If it turns out that it was a beneficiary, that beneficiary may have to return the item at the executor's request. If the item isn't returned, the executor may deduct its value from the beneficiary's inheritance.

97. Can the executor hold an estate sale or garage sale?

Yes, unless the will gives other instructions. The executor can dispose of household goods in any method that seems reasonable in the context of the will, the goods in question and the situation. Obviously any items that are specifically left to individuals must be given to them first, and only items that are not specifically mentioned may be sold in a garage or estate sale.

All proceeds of the sale must be put into the executor's estate bank account. The proceeds become part of the residue of the estate.

As a beneficiary, you might want to keep an eye on how household items are sold if there are antiques or artwork or family heirlooms in the sale. Executors should have obtained appraisals for any items that might be valuable. If an executor sells an item for much less than its actual worth, the executor may be held liable for the loss to the estate.

98. What is a Memorandum of Personal Effects?

A Memorandum of Personal Effects is a document, separate from a will, which describes how a person wants his or her personal and household goods to be distributed after his or her death. It is intended to be a supplement to a will, and not to replace a will. A Memorandum covers any personal items (jewelry, photo albums, clothing, collections) and household items (furniture, décor items, wall art, dishes) owned by the deceased, in all locations. This means the deceased's home, cabin, shed, garage or workshop.

A Memorandum does not give away sums of money or real estate. If it does, it may actually be a will or codicil, even if that isn't what the deceased intended.

Not everyone who makes a will decides to make a Memorandum. Sometimes people simply include the list of who gets what right in the will itself. Whether or not a Memorandum is appropriate is something that estate planners usually discuss with their clients so that the clients know their options.

Most of the time, people make up their own form of Memorandum simply by making a handwritten list of specific items along with the names of the people who will inherit those items. There are very few formal rules for a Memorandum; it should be signed and dated but it doesn't need witnesses.

There are two basic types of Memorandum of Personal Effects. One type is incorporated by reference into a will, and the second type is not. If a Memorandum is incorporated into the will, it is prepared and signed before the will is made, and is specifically mentioned in the will. It can't be changed unless the will is changed too. If it is not incorporated into the will, it can be signed and changed at any time before or after the will is signed.

99. If there is a Memorandum of Personal Effects, do we have to follow it?

A Memorandum of Personal Effects that is not incorporated into a will does not have the same legal force as a will. This means that all of the residuary beneficiaries must agree to abide by the Memorandum in order for it to be valid. This usually works well, but can be impossible if beneficiaries simply cannot get along.

100. The Memorandum of Personal Effects leaves me money, but the executor won't pay it to me. Why is that?

If a Memorandum gives instructions to give someone a sum of money, there is a problem. A Memorandum is by law restricted to giving away household and personal items. If there is a gift of money, it's possible that the Memorandum may replace the existing will, or act as a codicil. In a case like this, the executor should take the Memorandum and all other estate documents to an experienced lawyer to figure out the effect it will have. Don't expect to receive anything until the executor has a clear picture of the legal ramifications of the documents.

101. Don't personal and household items automatically get returned to the person who gave them to the deceased?

No. That's one of those common but unfounded misconceptions that has no basis in law.

102. My Mom had taped our names onto the back of certain items. Isn't that the same as making a Memorandum leaving us those items?

No. Legally this has no effect whatsoever. In certain places in Canada it seems to be almost universal that women put a piece of masking tape on the back of household objects and write someone's name on it. According to surviving family members, this supposedly indicates the name of the beneficiary of the object after the woman's death. However, there is no basis in law for this arrangement. If all of the residuary beneficiaries agree, they can choose to honour those pieces of tape, but there is nothing that a beneficiary can do to force them to do that.

103. My Mom told me verbally who is to get her household items. Is that legally binding?

No. Testamentary instructions must be in writing.

104. Do household contents automatically belong to whoever inherits the house?

No. If the person who is receiving the house is the spouse of the deceased and lived with the deceased at the time of death, he or she will most likely keep the household and personal goods. This is because they were being used by both occupants of the house and are considered to be jointly owned.

If a gift in a will states that a beneficiary is supposed to receive a house, this means the title to the property. It does not include the contents of the house unless the will also specifically says that the beneficiary gets the contents.

105. Is it fair for the estate to pay for appraisals of items, as opposed to this being paid for by the person who receives them?

Yes, this is fair. It is the job of the executor, not the beneficiary, to locate, identify and place a value on the assets of the estate. Therefore the estate must pay for any appraisals.

Chapter 9: Distribution of the Estate

The distribution of the estate is the payment or transfer of estate assets to the beneficiaries. This is an area in which beneficiaries often reveal themselves to be impatient, suspicious and aggressive. Much of the problem arises because beneficiaries are just not aware of all of the behind-the-scenes work that happens on an estate, and they tend to assume the executor is delaying things for no good reason. Executors often bring this on themselves by not communicating with the beneficiaries. This chapter is intended to shed some light on the process of distribution so that your anxieties may be kept under control.

106. When should I expect my inheritance?

Most estates are wrapped up in twelve to eighteen months, as long as there are no serious complications. Estates that have lawsuits or particularly complicated assets (such as businesses to wind down or overseas property to sell) take longer than more simple estates. If the executor is willing to do an interim distribution (see question 106 for more on that), then you will get your inheritance many months earlier than if the executor refuses to do this.

107. Why can't I get my money right away?

You will have to wait until the executor completes at least some of the estate work. The executor will generally have to get probate first, then start collecting in the assets. Until that time, the executor doesn't have any money to give you. After all, if the house isn't sold and the investments aren't cashed in, where is the money supposed to come from?

The executor is also bound by law to make sure that all debts, expenses and taxes are paid before the beneficiaries get anything. This alone can take some time, especially if there are claims to deal with. A claim could be made by a caregiver, supplier of medical goods, or the neighbour boy who cuts the grass. There could be disputed charges on a credit card. The varieties are endless, and the executor has to deal with all of them before any beneficiaries see any money.

The executor may want to wait until Canada Revenue Agency has given a final Tax Clearance Certificate that proves that all taxes are paid. The executor is well within his or her rights to do this. The more bickering and accusations that have occurred during estate administration, the more likely the executor will choose to protect himself by waiting for the Clearance Certificate before distributing to the beneficiaries. Getting that Clearance Certificate takes several months, and the waiting period can't even begin until the executor has wound up the estate, paid the taxes, and submitted an application form to Canada Revenue Agency.

108. What is an interim distribution?

An interim distribution is the process of distributing the bulk of the estate to the beneficiaries before the Tax Clearance Certificate is issued by Canada Revenue Agency. The vast majority of executors will choose to make an interim distribution.

The basic idea behind the interim distribution is that the executor, hopefully with the assistance of an accountant or lawyer, will hold back a portion of the estate. The holdback amount should be enough to pay any unpaid taxes, legal and accounting fees, and any other expenses. The executor then pays out the bulk of the estate that is not needed for the holdback.

When the executor wants to make an interim distribution, he should put together a full accounting of the estate (see question 150 for more on that) and circulate the accounting to all beneficiaries together with a Release document. If the beneficiaries approve of the accounting, they return their signed Releases to the executor, and he distributes the funds to them. If they don't approve and sign the Releases, he doesn't pay the money out to any beneficiaries.

The word "interim" suggests that it's not a final distribution and that there may be more funds to pay to the beneficiaries later (see question 109). If an estate is simple and is wound up quickly, and the executor believes there are no taxes to be paid, there may be no need for an interim distribution.

Most estates have only one interim distribution, but if there is a complicated estate in which assets are sold over many years, there may be more than one. This is always the executor's call, as he or she is the one who bears the risk of paying out funds without the Clearance Certificate.

109. Why does the executor hold back some money in an interim distribution, and do we beneficiaries eventually get that money?

The executor holds back money so that he or she will have estate funds available to pay final taxes and expenses. If an executor pays everything to the beneficiaries then finds out that there are still some taxes unpaid, the executor would likely have to pay those taxes out of his or her own pocket. If all of the holdback money is not used for taxes and final expenses, the remaining amount is divided among the beneficiaries according to the will.

110. The executor insists he won't do an interim distribution. Can he do that?

An executor is not obligated to do an interim distribution, but almost all executors will do them. If the executor is refusing, he or she may be concerned about family squabbles that might arise during the interim distribution. Alternatively, the executor may be concerned about having enough funds in the estate to pay debts and expenses.

111. A creditor is telling me that I have to pay my deceased's husbands debts myself. Is that true?

If the debt belongs solely to one person, then his or her spouse is not obligated to pay the debt. If it's a joint loan or joint credit card, both spouses are on the hook. Otherwise, the creditor will be listed on the estate inventory along with all other creditors, and paid from the estate when assets become available. In cases where there are not enough assets to pay everyone, creditors often try to get the spouse to pay.

There may be exceptions to this general rule. For example, if a husband and wife owned a home jointly, and the husband's creditor placed a lien against the house while the husband was alive, the wife is going to have to deal with that lien before transferring the title.

112. Can I get a loan from the estate against my inheritance?

On occasion, an executor will agree to provide a loan to a beneficiary, but this is rare. It complicates the book-keeping and may give rise to the perception of favoritism among other beneficiaries. Also, if the executor had estate assets available, he would likely do an interim distribution to all beneficiaries rather than make a loan to just one of them.

113. Mom made one sibling the beneficiary of everything and expected him to share, but he won't. Now what?

The beneficiaries other than the one named are probably out of luck. A direction in a will that says that everything is left to one person, and gives that one person discretion to distribute the assets as he sees fit, gives no legal rights to the other beneficiaries. After all, that one named beneficiary may use his or her discretion to keep everything, and that is within the bounds of what the will says.

On the other hand, there is a chance of having the estate split among family beneficiaries if the assets were not left under the will, but were actually put into joint names by the deceased with one of the children. Inter-generational joint property can be attacked by the other family members on the basis that it is not a true joint ownership and should be part of the estate. This will likely take a lawsuit, or at least the threat of one, to achieve.

Chapter 10: Tax

Taxation of an estate may be a shock to the beneficiaries when they find out that the estate they expect to inherit is significantly reduced by tax. This is not the fault of the executor, despite them being blamed most of the time; if the deceased owned taxable assets, the estate has to pay the tax.

The other area of concern for beneficiaries is the effect of an inheritance on their own financial situation. I have provided basic tax information here, but I must add this caveat: I am not an accountant. As an estate planning professional, my job is to alert you to possible tax issues and urge you to get advice about them. If you have specific questions pertaining to your personal tax situation, your best resource is an experienced accountant.

114. Am I taxed on my inheritance?

A Canadian resident inheriting from a Canadian estate is not taxed on what he or she inherits. However, if that inheritance earns interest or dividends or increases in value after the beneficiary receives it, of course the beneficiary is going to pay tax on that.

115. What taxes does the estate have to pay?

There is no "death tax". The Canadian government does not automatically take a fixed percentage of a deceased person's estate, despite persistent rumours to the contrary. Provincial governments take a portion of the estate in the form of a probate fee.

However, there are still significant taxes against an estate. Estates must pay capital gains tax if there has been an increase in capital property such as real estate or shares in privately owned companies (see more about capital gains tax in question 116).

An estate must also pay income tax owing if the estate has registered assets such as RRSPs or RRIFs. The law says that an individual's RRSP or RRIF is deemed to be cashed in at the time that person dies. All funds taken out of an RRSP or RRIF by the individual are taxed, so if it is deemed to be cashed all at once, the whole sum is taxable. This could mean as much as 40% of the RRSP or RRIF being lost to taxes.

116. What is capital gains tax, and how much is it?

Capital gains tax is a federal tax on the increase in value of an asset. The tax is payable at the time the asset is sold, transferred, or put into a trust or estate. This only applies to capital assets, which for most people are real estate and shares of private companies. The taxable amount is one half of the increase.

For example, let's say that Bill bought a house for $50,000. He owns it for years, and when he dies, his house is worth $500,000. The gain is $450,000 ($500,000 - $50,000). Half of that gain, or $225,000 must be included as income on Bill's final tax return.

The exception to the rule is that if the house in question is Bill's principal residence, he does not have to pay capital gains tax. All of us in Canada are entitled to own one residence on which we don't have to pay capital gains tax. If the house was Bill's cabin, or a rental property, or a house he bought for his daughter to live in, the tax would be payable.

117. If I'm inheriting my parents' cabin, do I pay tax on it?

If you live in Canada and you inherit something from an estate in Canada, you do not pay any tax on your inheritance. That seems a simple statement but in real life it can be confusing because, as described in question 116 above, there will be capital gains tax owed against the cabin if it increased in value while your parents owned it.

Even among people who realize there is tax against the cabin, the assumption made by many people is that the person who inherits the cabin pays the tax on the cabin. <u>This is not correct</u>. If there is capital gains tax owing on the cabin, this tax is paid out of the general residue of the estate, and not out of the share of the person who receives the cabin.

As an example, let's look at Joe's situation. He has a house worth $100,000 which he leaves to his son, Jack. He has a cabin worth $100,000 which he leaves to his daughter, Louisa. He leaves everything else to his son, Frankie. The "everything else" he leaves to Frankie includes Joe's bank accounts and his car, altogether worth $100,000. He believes he has treated his kids equally.

When Joe dies, Jack gets a house worth $100,000. Louisa gets a cabin worth $100,000. There is no tax on the disposition of Joe's house, but there is capital gains tax of $30,000 on the cabin. By law, that tax is paid out of the general estate, which in this case means Frankie's share. This means that Frankie will inherit $70,000, significantly less than his siblings.

This is an important point for beneficiaries to understand, as many people misunderstand this tax rule and become upset with the executor for taking the tax from the "wrong" person.

118. If I'm inheriting an RRSP, do I pay the tax?

If the deceased was your spouse, most likely the RRSP can be rolled over to you on a tax-deferred basis. This is usually the case, but check with the deceased's bank to be sure. Rolling over the RRSP means that no tax is payable right now, and there will be no tax until you take out the money or pass away. In limited situations, there can be a rollover to a dependent child.

If the RRSP (or RRIF) has been left to anyone else, there will be tax payable on the entire amount of the RRSP at the time it is paid to the beneficiary. However, the beneficiary is not the one who pays that tax. The tax is paid by the general estate, even if the beneficiary of the RRSP is not a beneficiary of the estate.

This rule causes a lot of confusion and a lot of disputes. You, as a residuary beneficiary, may have to pay tax on money that someone else received. Many people say it makes sense to them that the person who receives the asset should pay the tax. However, that is not how the tax rules work.

119. Are shares in my parents' company taxable when I inherit them?

Yes. Shares of private companies are considered to be capital property, so when the owner of the company passes away, the transfer of the shares is taxable. This is true whether the shares go directly to a beneficiary, or whether they go through the estate, or whether they are sold and the funds paid to the estate.

The tax in question is capital gains tax, which is a tax on half of the increase in value of a company. When a business owner started from scratch and built up a profitable company, the tax liability can be enormous. This tax hit goes on the deceased's personal tax return and not on the company's tax return.

The tax is paid from the residue of the deceased's estate. This means that one person can inherit the shares of the company, while another person who inherits the residue of the estate pays the taxes on the shares.

120. What's a tax clearance certificate?

A Tax Clearance Certificate is a document prepared by Canada Revenue Agency that certifies that all taxes payable by an estate have been paid. It is only issued when it has been requested by the executor or his or her accountant. The request is made once all tax returns for the deceased and the estate have been filed and all taxes have been paid.

It is not required by law that an executor apply for a Tax Clearance Certificate, so it's possible that the executor may choose not to get one. However, executors are almost always advised by their lawyers to get a Tax Clearance Certificate as proof that it is now safe to pay out the estate to the beneficiaries.

121. Should I believe the executor when he says he's still waiting for a clearance certificate?

I hear often from irate beneficiaries who are convinced they are being lied to by a conniving executor simply because the executor says, many months after probate, that the estate is at a standstill awaiting a clearance certificate. Though I'm sure in some cases the executor could be conniving, in the majority of cases the wait for the clearance certificate is very real. It takes several months and perhaps even a year to get a clearance certificate. The wait starts when the executor or the accountant applies for the certificate, not from the date of death or even the date of probate.

122. Will I be taxed when I later sell an inherited property?

It's important to realize that the tax does not attach to a specific asset; it applies against a specific transaction. If you inherit your parent's house, the estate doesn't pay tax because it was their principal residence. However, once you own it, it's got nothing to do with your parent's estate any more. It's not their principal residence any more so that tax-free status is completely irrelevant. Now it's your house.

If you already own a house of your own and you inherit a house from your parents, you may decide to sell the second house. If that house has increased in value and it's not your principal residence, then of course you will have to pay tax on it. It doesn't matter at that point whether you bought the house, inherited it or won it in a lottery. You are being taxed on the transaction of selling (or giving) the house.

Chapter 11: Trusts

Not every estate involves the share of a beneficiary being placed into a trust, but trusts are common enough that they deserve to be discussed in this Answer Book. A trust is a legal entity created by a legal document, but unfortunately most beneficiaries are given no legal information at all to guide them. This chapter should help you to understand what it means to have your inheritance held in trust, and what you should do to deal with it.

123. What is a trust?

A trust is any arrangement in which one person (the "trustee") holds on to money or property on behalf of someone else (the "beneficiary"). There are two basic kinds of trust. One is the testamentary trust, which is created by a will. The other basic kind is an *inter vivos*, or a trust that is set up while the owner of the assets is still alive.

124. How and when does a trust for me as a beneficiary get set up?

If we are talking about a testamentary trust, which is by far the most common type of trust, several things must happen before the trust is set up. First, the executor must obtain the probate order from the court. After that, there may be further delays if the trust is based on a portion of the residue of the estate. This is because the residue of the estate can't be defined until bills and debts are paid, and tax liability is calculated.

The executor sets up the trust and the beneficiary is not likely to be directly involved in this process at all. The executor will go to a trust company or bank, and make the necessary arrangements as set out in the will. Most likely you won't know about the arrangements until they are fully in place.

125. Is the executor in charge of all the trusts under the will?

Yes, this is the job of the executor, unless the will specifies otherwise. Sometimes testators like to put someone other than the executor in charge of a trust, for many reasons.

126. Why is my share in trust?

If your share is in trust, it is because the will directed it to be done that way. There are several reasons why your share might be in trust. The most common reasons are that the testator wanted you to reach a certain age before inheriting, or that the testator wanted to protect you from creditors. There are other possibilities too. The testator might have believed you need assistance handling money because you gamble, or have an addiction, or because your marriage is in trouble. Then again, some trusts are designed simply to give you some tax-planning options.

Finally, some trusts are set up so that the capital of the trust is preserved for another beneficiary to inherit after you pass away, particularly in blended families. The reason behind setting up the trust isn't always obvious from the will.

127. What if I don't agree that my inheritance should be held in trust?

In most cases, you are out of luck if you don't like your inheritance being held in trust. The trust was set up by the will, and does not require your consent or your co-operation. However, it is possible for a beneficiary to approach the court and apply for the trust to be collapsed. It's not an easy application nor one that is to be undertaken lightly. The simple fact that you don't want it to be in trust is not going to win in court.

128. How long will my share be in trust?

It will be held in trust for as long as the will specifies. It could be until you reach a specified age or meet a condition, or it could be in trust for your whole life. This is not up to the executor, who must follow the instructions in the will. Some wills contain permission for the executor to collapse the trust entirely and pay the money to you under certain conditions, such as the capital of the trust being so small as to be eaten up by money management fees.

129. How can I get money out of the trust?

You can receive money from the trust according to the terms of the trust itself. Those terms would have been specified in the will, so if you have a copy of the will you can read it to see what to expect in terms of receiving funds.

Though each trust is different, there are general rules that apply to all. The better the will, the better your trust is going to operate. To get a better understanding of your trust, look for the following items:

- The trust may specify that you are to receive a certain amount of money each month or each year;
- The trust may specify some condition that you have to meet before you receive anything, such as enrollment in post-secondary education, or reaching a certain age;
- The trust may allow for an encroachment, which means that you can sit down with the trustee to determine what funds you need and what is allowed by the will. For example, some trusts allow you to access funds if you need them for medical treatment, or for tuition. The majority of trusts allow funds to be used for what is referred to as the "maintenance and benefit" of the beneficiary. That is broad language that is used to keep the options

open as to what the beneficiary may need. An encroachment is only allowed if the trustee believes it to be a good idea;
- The trust may specify whether you have access to the capital of the trust, or only to the income earned on the capital;
- The trust may say that if the amount being held in trust becomes quite small, the trust can be closed and the money paid to you.

130. What kind of things can a trustee pay for when the will has a general power of encroachment for my benefit?

A power of encroachment in a trust means that the trustee can use some of the funds in the trust on behalf of the beneficiary (see the previous question for more detail on that). The usual wording for a power of encroachment is broad, and refers simply to the "benefit or maintenance" of the beneficiary.

This is generally considered to include medical expenses, school-related (including post-secondary) expenses and reasonable living expenses. The definition of what is "reasonable" depends on how much money is in trust, how long it must last, and whether anyone else is supposed to inherit the money after the current beneficiary. And, as always, the specific wording of the will has to be taken into account. For example, reasonable living expenses may include a vehicle if the trust is large, but not if the trust is small.

The ability of most executor/trustees to handle a trust and understand what is to be paid is a roll of the dice. People generally choose their executor/trustees because they are related to them, and don't put any thought at all into how they will handle a trust. Some trustees pay out the trust money so freely that it is spent long before the trust was supposed to end, and the beneficiaries receiving the funds tend not to object to this.

Other trustees are tight-fisted and refuse to pay for almost anything. In a case like this, a beneficiary will find it necessary to object.

A trustee who is doing his or her job properly will find the middle ground between frittering away trust money and controlling it too closely.

131. If the trust is for my kids, shouldn't it be paid to me to look after?

Not necessarily. The executor of the will is automatically the trustee of the trust unless the will gives other instructions. The fact that the beneficiary of a trust is a child does not change this. The specific wording of the will becomes important here, because wills vary in terms of how much leeway the executor has in dealing with the trust.

In some cases, paying the funds to a parent to look after is specifically forbidden in the will, particularly when the deceased was divorced from his/her children's other parent. In other wills, paying the trust fund to the parents to look after is specifically allowed.

132. If there is an ITF account that names me, when will I get this?

"ITF" stands for "in trust for". This is a type of bank account that anyone may set up. Although it contains the word "trust", it's not really a trust. On the death of the owner of the ITF account, the beneficiary named on the account will receive the funds, if the beneficiary is of the age of majority. If the beneficiary is still a minor, the executor will hold onto the account and pay it to the beneficiary when he or she comes of age.

133. What paperwork should I ask for if my inheritance is in trust?

I have found that beneficiaries' whose inheritance is held in trust usually receive very little in the way of paperwork. I believe this happens because the executor is focused on doing what the will asks him or her to do, and not so much on how things are perceived by individual beneficiaries.

A beneficiary for whom a trust is set up (or that beneficiary's legal guardian) should ask for additional paperwork in order to fully understand the terms of the trust. Getting a copy of the will is important, as it will contain the instructions for setting up the trust. If the beneficiary doesn't know and understand what the will says, he or she won't know whether the executor has done this correctly, or whether the trustee is conducting the trust properly.

There is a greater risk of funds disappearing when the beneficiary doesn't know what's going on.

A beneficiary in this situation has the right to know that his or her trust is being administered properly. Some people tell me they feel greedy when they insist on knowing when payments are to be made and how much the payments should be, but I don't see that as greedy at all. I see that as ensuring that a request made by the testator in his will is being properly carried out.

If the trust is being managed by a trust company, the beneficiary may request periodical accounting. These reports could be annual, semi-annual or quarterly, depending on whether there is activity in the trust. The beneficiary may also request these from any trustee, but non-professional executors frequently don't understand the obligation to provide ongoing accounting.

134. Do I pay tax on the money in the trust?

You don't personally pay tax on the money that is held in the trust, or the money that is paid to you from the trust. A trust itself is a taxpayer, so the trustee will have tax returns completed for the trust annually, and any tax owing is paid directly out of the trust.

There are exceptions to this rule, as it's possible to elect that tax on the funds in trusts be paid by the beneficiaries who receive payments.

135. If I get divorced, does my ex get half the money in my trust?

No. Funds held in a trust are the property of the trust, not the property of the individual beneficiary. Your funds should be safe from creditors or ex-spouses.

Chapter 12: Lawyers

Beneficiaries don't always get along with the estate lawyer. I believe this to be largely the result of the beneficiary thinking the lawyer works for him or her, and becoming exasperated when the lawyer won't answer questions or take instructions. I hope reading this chapter will clarify what a beneficiary should expect from the estate lawyer.

136. Must every estate have an estate lawyer?

No, there is no legal requirement that an estate be represented by a lawyer. However, most estates involve the legal system to the extent that letters probate or letters of administration must be obtained. Most executors are more comfortable asking a lawyer to handle the parts of an estate that go through the legal system.

If there is a legal dispute on an estate, such as someone contesting the will, the executor should always hire a lawyer for assistance.

137. Does the executor have to use the lawyer who drew the will to do the probate?

No. The executor is free to hire any lawyer he or she chooses for help with the estate.

138. What if the lawyer is friends with one of the other beneficiaries?

I've often been asked whether it's a conflict of interest to hire a lawyer who knows one of the beneficiaries or knows the executor. It is not a conflict, any more than it's a conflict to go to a dentist or a mechanic that someone knows. Lawyers are highly regulated, and are not likely to risk their license to practice law for every friend who hires them.

139. Will I have to help pay for the estate lawyer?

As a beneficiary, you won't be asked to come up with any money for the estate lawyer. However, the lawyer is paid from the estate, so if you are a residuary beneficiary, part of your share (and that of all other residuary beneficiaries) pays for the lawyer.

140. Who does the estate lawyer work for?

The estate lawyer works for the executor, not for the beneficiaries.

The estate lawyer may only accept instructions from his or her client, who is the executor. It would be impossible for a lawyer to try to accept instructions from every beneficiary on an estate.

141. Why does the estate lawyer keep telling me to talk to the executor?

Contrary to popular belief, it's the executor who is responsible for making decisions about what do to in an estate, not the lawyer. The lawyer's job is to inform and advise the executor, and then to carry out the tasks that the executor wants done. Also keep in mind that a lawyer working on the administration of an estate is being paid by the hour, so every time you call or email the lawyer, the cost goes up.

142. Do I need my own lawyer to protect my inheritance?

Generally, beneficiaries don't need their own lawyers to obtain their inheritance. However, sometimes it becomes advisable to hire your own lawyer. If you wish to dispute some aspect of the will or claim a greater share of the estate, you would need your own lawyer, as the estate lawyer cannot work against the estate he or she is already working for.

Beneficiaries sometimes like to consult lawyers when they receive the executor's accounting, as they want some guidance on whether the executor has acted properly. This is always open to a beneficiary, though the cost is paid personally and not from the estate.

143. The lawyer's bill for the estate was outrageous but the executor says he can't do anything about it. Is that true?

It's not necessarily true. When the executor hired the lawyer, he should have received a letter from the lawyer explaining how the lawyer planned to bill the estate. This explanation should include the amount to be billed, whether it was calculated on an hourly rate, exactly what work was to be done for the fee, and when the bill was to be paid. Lawyers don't usually take a retainer on a probate or estate administration file, but will bill their fee to the executor once the probate order has been granted.

If the executor felt that the lawyer was billing in a way that did not follow the original agreement, of course he could object to the bill. He and the lawyer could negotiate a settlement of the bill between them.

There is also a process known as "taxation of accounts" that is available to clients who feel that their lawyer has billed them too much. This is a court process carried on by an officer called a taxation officer. It involves both the lawyer and the client (in this case the executor) showing up at the same time to talk to the taxation officer. They would be required to bring any supporting paperwork, such as the initial letter mentioned above that sets out the terms of the billing arrangement. As the beneficiary is not the client, the beneficiary could not take the bill to taxation.

However, the beneficiary could make the executor aware of the process.

Taxation of accounts is not available everywhere, but where it is available, it is very effective.

144. If the lawyer is the executor, can he charge for legal work as well as an executor fee on the same estate?

Yes, he can, as those are two different jobs.

145. How much do lawyers charge to look after an estate?

The cost of hiring a lawyer to help with an estate can vary from hundreds of dollars to several thousand dollars. The main factor in determining what the lawyer will charge is what the executor asks the lawyer to do.

In some cases, the executor simply asks the lawyer to apply to the court for the probate order, then turn the order over to the executor. The executor will then finish the estate. If the work is restricted to that, the fee will likely be .05% to 1% of the estate.

On the other hand, the executor could ask the lawyer to take care of the whole estate. For this work, a lawyer will charge by the hour. This means the lawyer is going to charge by the hour for every phone call, every letter written, every meeting and every other task he or she does for the estate.

146. How much do trust companies charge for an estate?

All trust companies have an established fee schedule that may change from time to time. When a customer decides to name a trust company as his or her executor, he or she is quoted a fee for the trust company's work based on that fee schedule. Ideally, the customer and the trust company sign an agreement that sets out the fee, and this agreement is kept with the will. This way, everyone who is involved with the will after the customer passes away – i.e. his family, beneficiaries, estate lawyer, probate judge, accountant, and creditors – can see what the deceased agreed to pay to the trust company so there is no dispute.

A trust company will not exceed the provincial maximum allowed by law for executors and in fact in many cases will quote a fee well under the allowed amount.

147. If the lawyer is doing all of the work on the estate, does the executor still get a fee? That seems like double charging.

If the lawyer is doing some (or all) of the work that should be done by the executor, then the executor's fee should be reduced accordingly. Otherwise, paying both the lawyer and the executor would, in effect, be charging the estate twice for the same work.

The lawyer can charge legal fees for legal work done on the file. That normally involves applying for probate and all of the investigation and information gathering that precedes the probate application.

148. I was supposed to get something from my parent's estate but the lawyer didn't get the will done before my parent died. Can I do anything?

You might be able to. There is case law in Canada that puts the blame squarely on the lawyer for not getting a will prepared in a timely manner once the client gave instructions. What consists of a "timely manner" depends on the facts of each case. It will also depend on what efforts the lawyer made to get it done and signed. Sometimes, in fact more often than you might think, the delay is caused by the client himself or herself.

However, if you are very sure of your facts and can prove them, you just might have a case against the lawyer for the inheritance you didn't receive.

Chapter 13: The Executor's Accounts and Releases

When an executor is winding up an estate, he or she should provide an accounting to the beneficiaries. This rarely goes well. The problem is partly because executors think they are saving money by not getting professional help and provide accounts that are inaccurate, incomplete and sometimes completely misleading. Even well-meaning executors find it hard to produce a proper accounting.

The problem is compounded by the fact that beneficiaries don't know what the accounting is about either. A common lament that I hear is from a beneficiary who is upset that an executor is taking compensation or who believes that the executor sold the house for way too little. When I did a little deeper, I find that that beneficiary has signed a Release approving of these transactions, but doesn't even realize it. In other words, beneficiaries don't know what they are signing.

This chapter gives specific information about why you receive an accounting, what to look for, and what to do if it isn't acceptable.

149. When does the executor produce the accounting for the beneficiaries?

The executor should produce an accounting once the estate is all wound up. This means that tax returns have been filed, bills have been paid, assets that needed to be sold have been sold, and the executor is ready to pay the beneficiaries their shares of the estate. Most of the time this happens within a year of a person's death, but as estates vary widely, so does the timeline. It could be as soon as six months after death, or as long as two years. If there has been a lawsuit or dispute, of course it will take even longer for the estate to wind up.

In most estates, the executor proposes to do an interim distribution of the estate, which means that the executor is willing to pay out the bulk of the estate without waiting for the final tax clearance certificate. If so, the accounting is produced at the time of the interim distribution. If there is an accounting produced at the interim distribution, there is not usually another one done at the end of the estate.

150. What is the purpose of the accounting?

The purpose is to show the residuary beneficiaries what the executor has done with the assets and debts of the estate. It will also reveal the amounts spent on legal and accounting fees, as well as on expenses such as probate, land registration and other administrative matters. The accounting will also show the beneficiaries how much the executor proposes to take as his fee for looking after the estate. It will also show any specific gifts that have been paid out or given out, such as a payment of $1,000 to a charity, or giving the cabin to one of the kids.

Remember that residuary beneficiaries are the people who share the residue of the estate, which is basically whatever is left over after bills, expenses and specific gifts are paid out. The accounting is usually the first time the residuary beneficiaries get to find out exactly what "the rest of the estate" actually is.

There is usually quite a bit of information in an executor's accounting, and beneficiaries should take the time to compare the accounting to the inventory that was done at the beginning of the estate.

151. What should I be looking for when I review the accounting?

Reading an executor's accounting can be overwhelming. A good way to start is to look at the inventory of the estate that was done shortly after death, and trace each asset through the inventory. Here are a few tips:

- There should be a chronological listing of all money received by the estate (this usually means the executor's estate bank account)

and all expenses paid. If it is not chronological, it will be very hard to follow.
- There should be some form of reconciliation of accounts. This means taking the value of the estate at the time the person passed away, adding in all income, subtracting all expenses, and coming out with a value that is matched by current bank statements.
- There should also be a statement that shows how the executor is proposing to pay out the estate, based on the will. This must have actual dollar amounts, not just percentages.
- If there was a house in the estate, look through the accounting to see when the house was sold, for what amount the house was sold, and whether the sale proceeds were put into the executor's bank account. Check for items relating to a house, such as payment of property tax, the cost of an appraisal or the commission paid to a realtor.
- Look for capital gains tax on land or buildings that were not the deceased's principal residence. If you receive the accounting during an interim distribution, you may well find that the tax hasn't yet been paid, but that it's included in the amount listed as a "holdback". This refers to the amount that the executor expects to pay once the tax return is processed, and which he is holding onto for that purpose.
- Also trace through any GICs, bonds, Canada Savings Bonds, investment portfolios and mutual funds. You should be able to find in the accounting where the executor cashed in the deposit or bond and put it into the executor's account. You should also be able to

see any interest that was earned on these items.
- Look for funeral expenses. Make sure they seem right based on what you saw at the funeral, and that all expenses are listed.
- There should be several entries for bills paid on behalf of the deceased. You may be surprised by some of these items, as you may not have known that the deceased had a loan at the bank, or that the house was mortgaged, for example.
- Check the executor's math.
- Try to think of anything that is missing. For example, if you know the executor held a garage sale, or sold the deceased's car to a nephew, make sure you can find those things in the accounting.
- Check to see that the fee the executor is charging is in line with the will, or if not mentioned in the will, is reasonable.
- Look over the executor's expenses to ensure that he or she is only charging allowable items.

152. What if I don't agree with the accounting?

This is a huge problem area between executors and beneficiaries. The biggest problem is that beneficiaries let their emotions get the better of them. If they have any anger or resentment against the executor for any reason, this is the place where the beneficiaries usually choose to let it show. This is counter-productive.

The first thing you need to do is ask yourself what it is about the accounting that you don't like. Is information missing? And if so, is it information that you absolutely need to have to understand and process the accounting? Or are you just asking for the information so that you can give the executor a hard time?

In Canadian courts, judges are pretty fed up with beneficiaries and executors fighting over details to the extent that they become unreasonable. If a judge thinks that you're being petty or unreasonable, not only will he not grant your request for information, he may also order that you pay costs for the executor. Understand though, that the same goes for executors; they too must be reasonable.

Items that might be considered reasonable issues with the accounting are the omission of major transactions, under-valuation of assets, or an excessive claim for executor's compensation. Taking an executor to court because of a few dollars' difference is not reasonable.

Assuming your issue is a reasonable one, you should write to the executor (or have a lawyer do that, if you prefer) to state the nature of your objection. Calling on the phone or texting is not effective. Be as specific as possible. There is no point simply objecting to the whole thing just on principle. State your issue, and if possible, state what should be done to fix the problem.

153. What if the accounting just doesn't have all the information?

If an executor is working without an estate lawyer, you will more than likely have to ask for more information, as few executors get it right on their own the first time. You are entitled to ask for more information if you can't understand an entry in the accounting, or it seems to be out of whack with what you were expecting. Occasionally you might find that the executor has accidentally left something out, or has made an arithmetical error, or has put something in the wrong column. There is no reason you can't ask for those things to be corrected before you give your approval.

154. Is the accounting supposed to have all original receipts and invoices attached?

It is very rare that an accounting has original supporting paperwork attached. Unless you have good reason to need to see the originals, it really isn't reasonable to ask for them. Attaching original paperwork is unworkable in any event where there is more than one beneficiary who must receive an accounting.

155. What is a passing of accounts?

"Passing of accounts" refers to the process whereby the executor presents his accounting to the court, and the court reviews them. If the accounting is acceptable, the court will "pass" it. In most estates, accounts are not passed in the courts. Most of the time, the beneficiaries and the executor are able to come to an agreement on the executor's accounting and a passing of accounts is not required. If the beneficiaries refuse to approve the executor's accounts, the executor may apply to the court.

If an executor goes through the courts to pass his accounts, the cost of the lawyer is usually paid out of the estate.

156. Is it ok that the executor paid an accountant or lawyer to prepare the accounting rather than doing it himself?

This is perfectly alright, and in fact is preferable from a beneficiary's point of view. The executor is entitled to hire professionals such as lawyers, accountants, realtors, or appraisers to do the things in which the executor is not skilled. This is generally to the advantage of the beneficiaries as well, as the number of errors will be much lower when the documents are prepared by someone who has some experience with that kind of paperwork. Also, your average executor has no idea whatsoever what to put into an accounting and it can be frustrating for a beneficiary to have to keep asking the executor for better information.

157. What kind of actions on the part of the executor would reduce the executor's fee?

Anything done by the executor that caused a financial loss to the estate potentially reduces the fee that he may later collect. For example, an executor might sell an item too cheaply. For example, an executor might sell a piece of artwork for $50 when he should have sold it for $500. The difference ($450) should come out of the executor's fee.

If an executor keeps large amounts of cash for a long period of time in a safe deposit box or in an account that earns no interest, this causes a loss to the estate in the amount of interest that would have been earned had the funds been properly invested. The loss of interest income should come out of the executor's fee.

If an executor delegates parts of his job to the estate lawyer, his fee should be reduced as he has used his executor's fee to hire the lawyer. To be clear on this point, the executor's fee is not reduced by asking the lawyer to do the proper legal work on the estate; the executor's fee is only reduced if he asks the lawyer to do the tasks that the executor himself is supposed to do.

158. Is the executor allowed to claim expenses over and above his fee?

Yes, the executor is allowed to claim reasonable expenses that he incurs during the administration of the estate. An awful lot of executors seem to think that this should cover everything from their meals to their rent, but allowable expenses are a lot narrower than that. The executor's living expenses are not to be included, unless it's necessary for the executor to travel to take care of the estate. Even then, the expenses should be reasonable; there is no need for the executor to take executive class flights and order bottles of champagne to his hotel while on estate business (or if he does, let him pay for that himself). Meal expenses should be reasonable, and be only for the executor himself, and only when it's necessary for the estate that the executor pays for a meal.

Executors can charge for mileage while working on the estate. There is no set rate in law, but it seems reasonable to charge the same rate as the provincial government pays its workers for mileage. An executor can also cover his parking fees (but not parking tickets) for visits to the estate lawyer or accountant.

An executor cannot claim expenses for attending the funeral, even if he flies from out of town to attend. Neither can he pay for his family to attend, or for clothing to wear to the funeral. However, if the executor uses the same trip to deal with household goods, change the locks and visit the lawyer, for example, then those expenses may be claimed.

159. When do I get a Release?

You should expect to be asked to sign a Release near the end of the administration of the estate. This could well be a year after the deceased passed away, depending on how much work the executor had to do. You may get a Release earlier than that if the executor decides to do an interim distribution (see question 106 for more about interim distribution).

160. What is the purpose of the Release?

The Release comes with a set of documents (the executor's accounting) that are intended to show the beneficiaries what the executor has done with the assets and liabilities of the estate. Once the beneficiary has had a chance to read the documents and understand what has transpired in the estate, he or she signs the Release to show that he or she approves of the executor's actions up to that point. By signing the Release, the beneficiary is saying that he or she is satisfied with the accounting, which normally includes a statement of what the executor intends to take for his fee.

Once the Release is signed and returned to the executor, the beneficiary has given up any legal right to dispute any of the executor's actions that were covered in the accounting.

161. Are all beneficiaries asked to sign Releases, and are we legally required to sign?

Usually only the residuary beneficiaries of an estate are asked to sign Releases, but that is up to each executor. In fact, an executor can choose not to ask any beneficiaries to sign Releases, but to omit this step would go against legal advice offered by most lawyers. Many other executors get receipts for specific gifts (such as jewelry or household items) but don't ask the recipients of those gifts to sign a Release.

You, as a beneficiary, are not required by law to sign a Release. However, the Release document is an important part of a legal process. If you refuse to sign the Release, the executor has two options. The executor can work with you to find out what issues you might have with his or her accounting, and to resolve those issues so that you feel comfortable signing the Release. If that doesn't work or if for some reason this option is not going to be exercised, the executor's other option is to ask the court to pass the estate accounts. Once the accounts have been passed by the court, there will be no further need for you to sign a Release.

162. What other documentation should I expect to receive along with the Release?

You should receive enough information to understand what has happened with all of the assets and liabilities of the estate. There is no one set of forms that everyone has to follow, but the statements you get should include:

- The inventory of the estate that was done at the time of death (you may already have received that earlier when you received your notice);
- A statement of receipts and disbursements that shows when and how the executor collected in bank accounts, paid bills, sold the house, paid legal fees, etc. This is a

type of ledger that shows the various transactions. This particular item varies, as many executors will provide only a summary of transactions unless asked for more details;
- A statement that reconciles the inventory balances, all income and expenses, and the current bank balance;
- A statement of what the executor intends to claim as a fee, and as expenses;
- A statement showing how the executor intends to distribute the estate according to the will, or the administrator intends to distribute according to intestacy law. This should be an actual dollar amount, not just a percentage.

Do not expect to receive information about life insurance policies or RRSPs/RRIFs that were left to individual people, or about jointly owned property, as those assets are not part of the estate.

163. What if I sign the Release and then change my mind?

If you've signed the Release according to the proper form and have returned that Release to the executor, you are probably out of luck. You can ask for it back, but the executor may already have filed it at the court, or be unwilling to return it to you. The time to raise an objection to the accounting is before you sign the Release.

164. Does every executor ask for a Release?

No. It's up to each executor to decide whether he wants to do this. However, an executor who does not ask for Releases is leaving himself or herself open to a potential dispute of his or her administration of the estate. Without a Release, the executor could be brought to account for his or her actions on the estate at any time.

165. Why do I have to wait for everyone to sign off before I get my money?

As mentioned, the Release is accompanied by an accounting that sets out in specific dollar amounts what the executor proposes to pay out to each beneficiary. This proposal is based on the dollars currently available in the estate. If one of the beneficiaries disputes the accounting and the executor is required to pass his or her accounts in the court, the court costs come out of the estate. This reduces the available dollars in the estate, and the executor will have to re-work his or her accounting accordingly. If the executor has already paid out some of the beneficiaries using the earlier calculation, he or she will have over-paid and will have to try to recover the funds. It's much cleaner and easier simply to hold onto the funds until the executor knows how much each beneficiary is supposed to receive.

166. Can I withhold signing the Release if I don't like what is in the will?

The purpose of the Release is to agree with what the executor has done with the estate. The executor is not responsible for what the deceased said in the will, and has no control over what is in the will. Therefore, refusing to sign off on the executor because of something that isn't his responsibility makes no sense. If the executor had to by-pass your signature and apply to the court for a passing of accounts, and you stated that you would not sign the Release because of what is in the will, the court will pass the accounts and will likely tell you to pay the executor's legal costs as well.

167. Does my signed Release get filed at the court?

It's not required by law that an executor files the Releases at the court. Some do and some don't. When there is a lawyer involved, generally the lawyer will ensure that the Releases are filed, so that they don't become misplaced or damaged.

Chapter 14: Contesting a Will

Unfortunately, some estates do end up in court. In addition, when beneficiaries are disappointed or angered by something in a will, they sometimes threaten to contest. This chapter is intended to provide some information for beneficiaries that may clarify what would be involved should they begin a lawsuit against the estate.

168. What does it mean for a beneficiary to contest a will?

"Contesting a will" is a phrase that many people use to mean any lawsuit that involves anything to do with a will or estate. However, what it really means is a lawsuit that is intended to find the entire will invalid.

Not every lawsuit involving a will is really contestation. For example, neither a lawsuit to determine which beneficiary is entitled to a pension, nor a lawsuit to clarify the terms of a trust is trying to bring down the whole will. They are trying to work *with* the existing will. Even a beneficiary who petitions for a larger part of an estate is not trying to invalidate the will; that beneficiary's issue is only a change to the distribution.

It will take months and possibly even years for contestation litigation to conclude. It involves preparing legal documents, serving them on other parties, holding discoveries, and running a trial. Each of those steps has deadlines and waiting periods.

169. What are the grounds for contesting a will?

There are not very many grounds for trying to have a will declared invalid. They tend to be variations on the following themes:

- That the deceased didn't know what he or she was signing because of dementia, illness or injury that impaired his or her mental capacity to sign a will ("lack of testamentary capacity");
- That the deceased was coerced or influenced into making the will even though it wasn't what they really wanted to do ("undue influence");
- Problems with the document itself, such as lack of witnesses, improper witnesses, lack of signature.

170. If a clause in the will says I can't contest the will, is that valid?

These clauses are questionable. The case law that has accumulated in cases where this kind of clause was used is contradictory and confusing. The clauses are sometimes effective, and sometimes not.

The most important factor in these clauses is the wording. Even slight variations make a difference. One item that must appear in the clause in order for it to be valid, but which is often missing, is an alternate beneficiary of the inheritance that the contesting person is now not going to get. For example, if a clause says that Sean can't have his inheritance if he contests the will but doesn't say who gets it instead of Sean, the clause is not valid, and Sean can contest the will if he wants to (assuming he has a real reason for doing so).

171. How do I go about contesting a will?

You must have a lawyer to contest a will. It's simply too complicated to do on your own. You should find a lawyer with some expertise in estate litigation, and bring all of the paperwork you have that relates to the estate. Explain to the lawyer in detail why you want to contest the will. You may or may not have a case.

If the lawyer is going to take your case, be prepared to pay a hefty retainer, as contesting a will is time-consuming and intense, and rarely does a lawyer commence litigation without a retainer.

172. Will the Public Trustee contest a will for me?

No. It's not the role of the Public Trustee to act as a lawyer for people contesting wills. The exception to this rule would be if the Public Trustee is acting as your trustee because you are incapacitated in some way.

Sometimes the Public Trustee contests a will without anyone in the family asking them to do so. This is because the Public Trustee represents beneficiaries of an estate who are minors, and they want to ensure that children are given an appropriate share of an estate.

173. Who is allowed to ask the court for a larger share of an estate?

In all jurisdictions in Canada, there is law that says that certain people automatically have the right to ask for more from an estate than is left to them in a will. This also applies to situations where the deceased has passed away without a will and local laws state who is to get the estate, and in what proportions. This kind of application to the court to get more from an estate by one of these people is often referred to by lawyers and the courts as "dependent relief".

There are three classes of people who are automatically entitled to dependent relief. They are:
- a. A spouse of the deceased
- b. A minor child of the deceased
- c. An adult child of the deceased who has a mental or physical handicap that prevents him or her from earning a living.

Note that the definition of "spouse" changes from province to province. Common law spouses are allowed to claim dependent's relief in some places but not in others.

In order for one of these claimants to be successful in persuading a court to change the distribution under a will, the claimant must show that the will (or intestacy provisions) did not adequately provide for the claimant. It's important to understand that although the right to make the claim is automatic, the right to win in court is not. A claimant still has to prove his or her case to the judge.

174. If I contest the will, is my lawyer paid out of the estate?

The payment of costs is decided by the judge who hears the case. There was a time when pretty much all estate litigation was paid for out of an estate, but those days are gone. The general rule now is much like the rule for any other kind of lawsuit: the loser pays the costs for the winner. Therefore, if you contest the will and you lose, you could well end up paying your own legal costs as well as that of the estate. On the other hand, if you win, at least some of your costs will likely be covered.

175. Does the estate pay for the executor's lawyer if we sue the executor?

The general rule is that executors are fully indemnified from the estate for their actions. This usually translates into their lawyer being paid from the estate for things like interpretation of a will, or asking a judge for guidance on a tricky estate matter. However, this general rule only goes so far. If you are suing the executor for some wrongdoing, such as embezzlement, and you are successful, the estate is certainly not going to pay for that lawsuit.

Conclusion

Thanks for reading this book. I sincerely hope that you have found some of the answers you need.

I realize that the possible variations in fact situations are endless, and that there is no "normal" estate. However, I based the questions and answers in this book on the questions I hear most often so I hope to have covered most situations for most people. From here, you should be able to narrow down your research, or go to a meeting with an executor, lawyer or accountant much better prepared than you were before.

I always welcome questions, suggestions or other feedback from readers on my blog at www.estatelawcanada.com .